Theory and Practice of _____

CREATIVITY
MEASUREMENT

Theory and Practice of _____
CREATIVITY MEASUREMENT

EDITED BY

EUNICE M. L. SORIANO DE ALENCAR, PH.D.

MARIA DE FÁTIMA BRUNO-FARIA, PH.D.

DENISE DE SOUZA FLEITH, PH.D.

PRUFROCK PRESS INC.
WACO, TEXAS

Library of Congress Cataloging-in-Publication Data

Alencar, Eunice M. L. Soriano de.
 Theory and practice of creativity measurement / by Eunice M. L. Soriano de Alencar, Maria de
Fátima Bruno-Faria, and Denise de Souza Fleith.
    pages cm
 Includes index.
 ISBN 978-1-61821-160-6 (pbk.)
 1. Creative ability. 2. Creative thinking. 3. Creative ability--Study and teaching--Methodology.
 4. Creative thinking--Study and teaching--Methodology. I. Title.
 BF408.A454 2014
 153.3'50287--dc23
                                    2013047628

Edited by Bethany Johnsen

Cover and layout design by Raquel Trevino

ISBN-13: 978-1-61821-160-6

Printed in the United States of America.

At the time of this book's publication, all facts and figures cited are the most current available.
All telephone numbers, addresses, and website URLs are accurate and active. All publications,
organizations, websites, and other resources exist as described in the book, and all have been
verified. The authors and Prufrock Press Inc. make no warranty or guarantee concerning the
information and materials given out by organizations or content found at websites, and we are
not responsible for any changes that occur after this book's publication. If you find an error, please
contact Prufrock Press Inc.

Prufrock Press Inc.
P.O. Box 8813
Waco, TX 76714-8813
Phone: (800) 998-2208
Fax: (800) 240-0333
http://www.prufrock.com

TABLE OF CONTENTS

INTRODUCTION

We are pleased to offer readers a new book in the area of creativity that focuses on an issue that is attracting and challenging the scholars of this phenomenon: its measurement or assessment. The main factor that mobilized us to organize the book was the growing demand for permission, by professionals from several areas, to use instruments developed by us that we have cited in our publications. (The appendices to this book print our instruments in full for the reader's use.) A second factor was the perception of a scarcity of publications in Brazil addressing the measurement of creativity. Although excellent texts related to creativity are already available in the country, offering a rich source of information about different elements that are associated with the expression of creativity in different contexts, the question of its measure has not been discussed extensively enough in the literature available in several countries.

Chapter 1: The Measurement of Creativity: Possibilities and Challenges presents an overview of different categories of measures, such as the main tests of creative thinking, instruments to identify interests, personality traits, cognitive styles that are associated with creativity, procedures for assessing the degree of creativity of a product, and alternate ways to identify the level of an individual's creative abilities. It also addresses some parameters to be considered when evaluating the quality of the available instruments, as well as the steps to be taken in their application and interpretation.

Chapter 2: Obstacles to Personal Creativity Inventory describes an instrument that allows for assessment of the main barriers that limit the expression of the individual's creative potential. Its premise is that awareness of these inhibiting factors may result in changes that facilitate overcoming them. The full instrument can be found in Appendix A: Obstacles to Personal Creativity Inventory.

Because of the importance that has to be given to education, especially in Brazil, where few have access to higher education, turning attention to creativity in the classroom becomes a key issue. Thus, in Chapter 3: Assessment of the Climate for Creativity in the Classroom, we present a tool for assessing a classroom's climate for creativity. This instrument aims to identify factors that facilitate or inhibit the expression of creativity in the school context. It can be used for diagnostic purpose of the climate for creativity in the classroom, especially in elementary school. Based on this diagnosis, intervention strategies can be devised in order to promote favorable conditions for the development of creative potential in the classroom. The full instrument can be found in Appendix B: Classroom Climate for Creativity Scale.

Continuing the focus on education, Chapter 4: Inventory of Teaching Practices for Creativity in Higher Education presents a tool that allows the evaluation of the perception of college students of the extent to which creativity has been encouraged by their professors. Such an evaluation may contribute to changes in teaching practices that could facilitate the creative expression of students and faculty. The full instrument can be found in Appendix C: Teaching Practices Inventory.

Returning to a more specific aspect of education, Chapter 5: Assessment of Creativity in Mathematics presents a test of creativity in mathematics. Because it is a discipline in which students often have difficulties, this measure can help identify gaps to be minimized in the teaching of mathematics, so that this discipline can be a fertile space for the expression of creativity.

The final two chapters focus on specific measures in the organizational context. The Indicators of Climate for Creativity (ICC), which is an instrument that identifies a set of incentives and barriers to creativity in the workplace, is described in Chapter 6: Indicators of the Climate for Creativity in the Workplace, and printed in Appendix D: Indicators of the Climate for Creativity in the Workplace. Also, in order to facilitate its management in organizational contexts, Chapter 7: Strategies for Creating at Work presents a measure to assess creative strategies in the workplace, printed in Appendix E: Creative Strategies at Work. When aware of the strategies used by professionals at work, managers can trace strategic actions that facilitate the expression of creativity.

It is noteworthy that, in addition to describing the process of construction and validation of instruments, we present these instruments in their entirety. This makes it possible for interested professionals to use the different measures in their research or in their work practice, contributing not only to the advancement of knowledge about different aspects of creativity, but also to its flourishing in diverse environments.

Eunice M. L. Soriano de Alencar
Maria de Fátima Bruno-Faria
Denise de Souza Fleith

CHAPTER 1

THE MEASUREMENT OF CREATIVITY

POSSIBILITIES & CHALLENGES

Eunice M. L. Soriano de Alencar, Denise de Souza Fleith,
and Maria de Fátima Bruno-Faria

The primary objective of this chapter is to discuss key aspects related to measures of creativity. It initially gives a brief history of studies of this construct, pointing out factors that prompted interest in its investigation, besides highlighting recent theoretical contributions and benefits of the development and use of procedures to measure various facets of creativity. Some main measurement instruments that have already been developed are listed in the text. The chapter also describes technical issues to be considered by those interested in making better use of the available assessment instruments of creativity, signaling their limits, possibilities, and also the precautions that should be taken in both the application and interpretation of their results. It's expected to be a source of inspiration for researchers in the area, unveiling new possibilities for research and for the promotion of conditions conducive to the development and expression of creative potential.

As widely reported in previous texts (Alencar, 2007; Alencar & Fleith, 2003b; Cropley, 2006; Nakano & Wechsler, 2007; Oliver, Shah, McGoldrick, & Edwards, 2006; Smith-Bingham, 2006), the importance of creativity in diverse contexts has been increasingly recognized, given its benefit not only for the individual but for society as well. As pointed out by Smith-Bingham (2006):

> The future prosperity of developed and developing countries will increasingly depend on their capacity to innovate, to develop ideas into new products and services, to develop new technologies and new forms of production, to introduce products and services to new markets (p. 11).

Brief History of Studies on Creativity

The interest of psychology in the study of creativity and the conditions that favor its expression is relatively recent. This interest had its most significant starting point in the 1950s, as the result of several factors, such as the influence of the humanist movement. Rogers (1959) and Maslow (1959), for example, pointed to the human potential for self-actualization, describing the conditions that facilitate the expression of creativity, besides drawing attention to mental health as a source of creative impulses. Moreover, they conceived creativity as the result of a mutually beneficial interaction between the person and the environment. Rogers also considered autonomy and the resistance to excessive social control as necessary conditions for creative activity. Rogers signaled the role of society, allowing the person freedom of choice and action, as well as recognizing and encouraging the individual's potential to create.

Another factor that contributed to arousing the interest of psychologists was the speech of Joy Paul Guilford upon assuming the presidency of the American Psychological Association in 1950. On that occasion, Guilford (1950) drew attention to the neglect of research on creativity by American psychologists, noting that among the 121,000 titles indexed in *Psychological Abstracts* to that year, only 186 had to do with creativity. In his speech, Guilford stressed the importance of social creativity, especially in finding new solutions to the problems facing humanity, and pointed to the need for a systematic study of its many facets.

From that moment on, different aspects associated with creativity have become the subject of numerous investigations, which have traditionally been classified in the following categories: person, process, product, and context (Runco, 2004). The first category includes studies related to personal characteristics, such as, for example, cognitive abilities, personality traits, motivation, learning styles, and creativity styles. The second, process, includes studies on operations and strategies that a person uses to generate and analyze ideas, solve problems, make decisions, and manage his or her thinking during the creative process. Studies have also been conducted on the properties of a product characterized as creative, especially in relation to its degree of originality and relevance. Context, the fourth category of research on creativity, includes elements of the culture in which creative activity occurs, such as values and norms prevailing in a given society, as well as other specific variables of the environment closest to the individual, such as the psychological climate of the workplace, physical environment, and available resources—human, financial, and even the time needed to develop and implement new ideas.

In relation to context, it should be noted that studies of creativity in the workplace have gained greater importance. An increasing number of investigations on creativity in organizations have taken place in the last 10 years. At the same time, different theoretical and methodological approaches were proposed to better understand creativity at work, especially as a means of promoting organizational innovation (Zhou & Shalley, 2008).

In recent theoretical approaches, such as the Investment Theory of Creativity (Sternberg, 2003; Sternberg & Lubart, 1995, 1996), the Componential Model of Creativity (Amabile, 1983, 1996b), and the Systems Perspective (Csikszentmihalyi, 1988, 1996, 1999), different factors that contribute to the creative expression are determined, including both personal variables that facilitate or constrain the expression of creativity and social, cultural, and historical elements that interfere in creative production, which interact among them in complex ways (Alencar & Fleith, 2003a, 2003b). Futhermore, according to these theoretical approaches, the individuals who stand out for their creative output rarely work in a vacuum, isolated from the social systems that constitute its domain of activity. Accordingly, Csikszentmihalyi and Sawyer (1995) consider that many elements of the social context are present in different stages of the creative process, creativity being a psychosocial phenomenon whose expression is the result of both the individual and characteristics of his or her social environment or ecosystem. Montuori and Purser (1995) summarized this idea, arguing that creativity is as much a social as an individual phenomenon, and requires an interdisciplinary, historical, ecological, and systemic approach.

In parallel to the studies with respect to the different elements that are associated with creativity, a large variety of definitions emerged in the literature. Nine years after Guilford's speech drawing the attention of psychologists to the need for research in the area, Taylor (1959) counted more than 100 different definitions of creativity—definitions that were often conflicting, emphasizing different aspects of the phenomenon. This is certainly due to the fact that creativity, like intelligence, is a complex, dynamic, and multidimensional construct. These characteristics justify the difficulty of achieving a precise definition and explain the reason for the many conceptions already proposed for the term, which have prioritized different aspects, such as characteristics of the individual, creative processes, creative elements in the product, or environmental factors associated with creative expression.

Advantages of the Development and Use of Measures of Creativity

A misconception about creativity that dominated psychologists' thinking by the middle of the 20th century was the view that creativity is a magical and mysterious phenomenon, difficult to define and even more difficult to measure. It was also believed that the concept of intelligence was sufficient to explain all aspects of mental functioning and that intelligence tests could measure any process that occurs in the mind (Getzels & Csikszentmihalyi, 1975). It was believed that intelligence could apply to any person, but creativity was the prerogative of only a privileged few. The measurement of intelligence was accepted and valued; IQ, as a measure of intelligence, was widely known, perpetuating the idea that intelligence was a dimension easily evaluated. In regard to creativity, on the other hand, opposing ideas prevailed. Only in recent decades has the importance of instruments to measure creativity been perceived. It was concluded that, in order to expand our understanding of the phenomenon in its complexity and multiple dimensions, measurements would be fundamental. The advantages of their development and use began to be signaled. The advantages of measurements for creativity included (Treffinger, 2003):

- helping people recognize and affirm the strengths and talents of individuals and enabling people to know and understand themselves;
- expanding and enhancing the understanding of the nature of human abilities and giftedness;
- providing "baseline" data for assessing individuals or groups, guiding teachers in planning and conducting appropriate and challenging instruction;
- providing pretest and posttest data for group comparisons for research or evaluation;
- helping instructors, psychologists, or individuals discover unrecognized or untapped talent resources;
- providing a common language for communication among professionals about the nature of creative abilities and skills;
- helping to remove creativity from the realm of the mystery and superstition; and
- providing operational constructs to help advance theory and research on creativity. (p. 60)

Besides these advantages, others highlighted by Torrance (cited in Cramond, 1999), include:

- promoting understanding of the human mind, its functioning and development;
- assisting in the development of individualized instruction;
- providing additional information in remediation and psychotherapy programs;
- evaluating differential effects of materials, programs, curricula, and educational programs; and
- identifying potential that remains ignored, especially in children and young people from culturally disadvantaged environments. (p. 308)

The Different Types of Creativity Measures

A review of the literature related to creativity measures indicates an increasing number of instruments built with the aim of collecting data on the multiple dimensions of the construct, and of investigating variables that influence the expression of creativity in diverse environments. These instruments have been classified in different categories by different authors. Callahan (1991), for example, classified them into three groups: performance/product, personality/attitudes/values, and biographical inventories. Piirto (1999) described five categories: (a) projective measures, (b) measures of personality, (c) measures of divergent production, (d) checklists and inventories, and (e) consensual assessment of products. On the other hand, Hocevar and Bachelor (1989), after examining more than 100 different measures of creativity, classified them in the following categories: (a) tests of divergent thinking; (b) attitude and interest inventories; (c) personality inventories; (d) biographical inventories; (e) ratings by teachers, peers, and supervisors; (f) judgments of products; and (g) self-reported creative activities and achievements. Besides these, Hocevar and Bachelor also included the study of eminent individuals, which, in our view, does not constitute a kind of measure since, in these studies, different methods of evaluation and assessment have been used, ranging from tests of creative thinking and biographical inventories to clinical interviews and portfolio analysis.

Tests of Creative Thinking

Among the various types of measures, the tests of divergent thinking (also called creative thinking) are probably the best known. It is noted that the first tests of this nature were developed by Guilford (1950, 1967) about six decades ago, when he was conducting studies in respect to intelligence. According to his investigations, IQ tests could not predict capacity for innovation and originality. His studies culminated in the construction of a theoretical model of human intelligence, named by him as Structure of the Intellect, which originally included 120 different factors. Among the various intellectual operations proposed by Guilford and included in this model was divergent thinking. This operation refers to the production of numerous alternative responses to a question, and contrasts with convergent thinking, which requires only one response from a single individual.

Among Guilford's contributions were the various tests he proposed to measure the different abilities related to divergent thinking and other abilities that contribute to creativity. Guilford hypothesized that there would be at least eight primary abilities underlying creativity, many of them related to divergent thinking. Among them could be cited: (a) fluency, which refers to the ability to generate many ideas or responses to a given problem; (b) flexibility, which implies changes, either in meaning, interpretation, or use of something in the strategy of doing a task, or even in the direction of thought; (c) originality, identified by the presence of unusual or remote responses, being the criterion of statistic rarity used to determine the degree of originality of the answer in a certain population; (d) elaboration, which refers to the ability to add a variety of details to a piece of information, a product, or a scheme; (e) redefinition, which implies transformations, revisions, or other forms of changes in the information; and (f) sensitivity to problems, which is the ability to identify defects or deficiencies in a situation, object, or institution. Guilford also highlighted that, although divergent thinking abilities are those that are more directly involved in creative thinking, all types of factors represented in the Structure of Intellect could contribute to the creative process at some point.

Examples of tests proposed by Guilford to examine some creative thinking abilities are:

- Associative fluency: The individual is requested to write several sentences of four words, each word beginning with a K, a U, a Y, or an I.
- Alternative uses: The examinee must list as many uses as possible for a particular object (e.g., a newspaper).
- Consequences: The individual is asked to write consequences of a given hypothetical event (e.g., what if people no longer needed to sleep?).
- Unusual uses: The respondent is asked to name the largest possible number of unusual uses for a common object (e.g., a brick).

Other examples of tasks to assess various factors associated with divergent production and other operations included in the Structure of Intellect

Model, which contribute to creative expression, were recently presented by Michael (2003).

A battery of tests of creative thinking also widely used, both in research in different countries and in the process of identifying gifted students to participate in special programs, are the Torrance Tests of Creative Thinking (Torrance, 1966, 1974). According to Cramond (1999), these tests have already been translated into more than 30 languages, with more than 2,000 studies with its use up to the beginning of the last decade. This battery includes a verbal part with seven tests and a figural part with three tests, both with two distinct forms. The battery aimed, in its original version, at assessment of four dimensions of creativity: fluency, flexibility, originality, and elaboration. Later, other dimensions started being scored, such as, for example, movement, fantasy, and unusual perspective. The test was validated and adapted to the Brazilian culture by Wechsler (2002, 2006a).

In one of the verbal tests of the Torrance Battery, the examinee is shown a picture and asked to write the largest possible number of questions about what is happening in the picture. In another verbal test, the respondent is requested to suggest changes to a toy in order to make it more attractive and interesting to children. In Picture Completion, one of the figural tests, the examinee should complete each picture, drawing a figure or object. In Circles, another figural test, 36 identical circles are presented, with instructions to the respondent to make different drawings with each of the circles.

Fluency is scored by counting the number of relevant responses given in each test. Flexibility is evaluated by the number of different categories in which answers can be sorted. Originality is scored based on the statistical frequency of each response. Elaboration is scored counting the number of details present in each response.

The Test for Creative Thinking – Divergent Production (Urban & Jellen, 1996) is another test that has been used both in research conducted in different countries and as a criterion in the identification of gifted students for educational programs. This test is restricted to figural creativity and is presented in two forms. The respondent receives a sheet of paper containing figural fragments and is instructed to make a drawing (or drawings) using these fragments. Fourteen dimensions are assessed by the test, including, among others, humor and affectivity, new elements, perspective, connections made with a line, and connections made to produce a theme.

Interests, Personality, Biographical, and Cognitive Styles Inventories

Although the tests of creative thinking are probably the most widely used instrument in research and the most discussed in the literature on creativity measurement, other types of instruments were also developed to assess the psychological traits, personalities, motivation, biographies, interests, and styles of creativity that in general characterize the most creative people. The interest inventories fall into this category; for example, the Group Inventory for Finding Creative Talent (GIFT), the Group Inventory for Finding Interests (GIFF I and GIFF II), and the Preschool and Primary Interest Descriptor (PRIDE), developed by Davis and Rimm (1982) and Rimm, Davis, and Bien (1982). Some items illustrative of these instruments are: (a) I have sense of humor, (b) I have a large variety of hobbies, (c) I like writing stories, and (d) I like trying new approaches to solve a problem. The different items are answered on a five-point scale, including "no," "to a small extent," "to some extent," "above average," and "definitely."

Several other instruments to identify attitude and interest were developed and have also been cited in studies conducted in the area. However, an analysis of their items indicates that some of them seem to assess personality traits, such as self-confidence (e. g., I have confidence in my intellectual ability), and curiosity (e.g., I am very curious).

A description of available instruments to measure motivation and favorable attitudes to creativity is presented by Cropley (2005). Among other instruments, the author points to the Creativity Attitude Survey and Basadur Preference Scale, which include a set of items related to attitudes regarding creativity, the first validated to be used with children and adolescents and the second with adults. Such instruments have been used in addition to tests of creative thinking, allowing a more complete picture of the psychological prerequisites for creative production.

Personality inventories and checklists are also described in the literature. These inventories and checklists have been used especially by researchers who characterize creativity as a set of personality traits rather than cognitive traits (Hocevar & Bachelor, 1989). A variety of items integrate these instruments with the purpose of identifying the extent to which the individual presents traits associated with creativity, such as autonomy, self-confidence, initiative, perseverance, spontaneity, emotional sensitivity, etc. In Brazil, a checklist of this sort was developed by Alencar (1998), who used it in a study with outstanding researchers with respect to their creative output. This checklist includes, among others, the following attributes: enthusiasm, flexibility, initiative, independence of thought and action, imagination, and willingness to take risks.

Also Torrance, who is best known for his tests of creative thinking, developed the instrument What kind of person are you? (Torrance & Khatena, 1970), which falls into the category of personality tests. It requests the respondent to select adjectives to describe him or herself in a forced-choice format. Pairs of adjectives are presented to the individual, who must select the one that best applies to him or her. Three sample items are: "prefer to work alone" or "prefer to work in groups"; "determined" or "obedient"; and "imaginative" or "critical, polite." The authors believe that creative individuals tend to describe themselves, for example, as more imaginative than polite, as a person of initiative rather than obedient.

Another measure developed by Khatena and Torrance (1976) was the Khatena-Torrance Inventory of Creative Perception – Something About Me. In this scale, respondents are asked to read through a list of statements and tick those that apply to them. Examples of statements are: "I am an imaginative person, a dreamer or a visionary," "I invented a new product," "Others consider me eccentric," and "When confronted with problems, I try to think of original ideas."

Biographical inventories, with a wide variety of items relating to hobbies, interests, activities during childhood, creative production in the early years, educational history, and family history, are also described, especially in the U.S. literature. According to Amabile (1983, 1996b), most of these inventories were originally developed on an intuitive basis and refined by testing samples of individuals considered more and less creative.

Cognitive styles refer to how an individual generates new ideas (Lubart, 2007). Several instruments were developed to assess this aspect, such as the Kirton Adaptor-Innovator Inventory (Kirton, 1987) and Thinking and Creation Styles (Wechsler, 2006b). The first one is based on the adaptation-innovation theory, proposed by Kirton, which assumes that any individual can be located on a continuum that ranges from the ability to "make things better" to the ability to "do things differently." Those with an adaptive preference are characterized as dependable, precise, efficient, disciplined, attentive to norms, and methodical. On the other hand, those with an innovative preference are usually individualistic, spontaneous, undisciplined, rule-breakers and, when faced with a problem, are inclined to reorganize it or restructure it, with less predictable responses and a greater degree of originality. The Kirton Adaptation-Innovation Inventory includes 32 items that identify a preferred style of creativity by an individual. It has been widely used in research in different countries, including Brazil (Gimenez, 1993).

According to Wechsler (2006b), "the evaluation of styles of thinking and creating allows one to know the individual's creative potential to produce and to be outstanding in many different areas" (p. i). Styles are preferred ways of thinking and behaving when faced with certain situations. The Thinking and Creation Style Inventory assesses three main styles—cautious reflexive, nonconformist transformer, and logical objective thinking—and two secondary styles—emotional intuitive and relational divergent. One hundred items comprise this instrument, which are answered on a six-point scale ranging from "strongly disagree" to "strongly agree." Examples of items include the following.

- I like to work following instructions.
- I am a conformist.
- Even if I fail, I love and believe in the importance of what I do.
- I am open to new ideas.
- I make decisions intuitively.
- I make decisions based on my feelings.
- I am an objective person.
- I prefer to make decisions based on logical thinking.
- I respect the right of others to make decisions.
- I like texts that use poetic language.

Ratings by Teachers, Peers, and Supervisors

An alternative method of identifying the individual's creativity is through nomination by teachers, peers, or supervisors, who are requested to rate their students', peers', or employees' level of creativity. Especially in studies conducted in the educational setting, teachers have been frequently requested to inform on the level of creativity of their students. One of the instruments for teachers available in the literature is the Teacher Evaluation of Creativity Sheet (Torrance, 1966). This instrument requires the teacher to list the five most and five least fluent students in their class, the five most and five least flexible, the five most and five least original, as well as the five best students at elaborating ideas and the five least able to elaborate ideas. In the instructions, the respondents are informed of the meanings of "fluency," "flexibility," "originality," and "elaboration."

Torrance developed this instrument based on previous studies (Torrance, 1962, 1963) in which he found that teachers were able to evaluate the students' creative abilities, provided they received an adequate description of creative behavior. Torrance's results indicated that students nominated as most fluent, flexible, original, and elaborative in their thinking and those nominated as the least fluent, flexible, original, and elaborative in their thinking had been differentiated by appropriate scores on the Torrance Tests of Creative Thinking. However, both Alencar (1974b) and Rush, Denny, and Ives (1967) found little agreement between teachers' rating and the results on creative thinking tests. Studies also showed that the validity of teachers' and other professionals' ratings significantly increased when the rating was preceded by a training of the evaluators (Johnson & Fishkin, 1999).

Renzulli et al. (2000) also constructed scales for the Assessment of Behavioral Characteristics of Students with Superior Abilities to be used by teachers to assess students in different areas, such as creativity, learning, motivation, leadership, arts, music, theater, communication, and planning. In Brazil, these scales have been used in the identification process of gifted students for special programs. The following items illustrate the scale content related to creativity (Renzulli et al., 2000):

The student
- generates a large number of ideas or solutions to problems and questions;
- displays a great deal of curiosity about many things, and is constantly asking questions about anything and everything;
- is a high risk taker, adventurous, and speculative;
- displays a keen sense of humor and sees humor in situations that may not appear to be humorous to others;
- generates a large number of ideas or solutions to problems and questions; and
- often offers unusual, different, unique, and clever responses.

The subjective judgment has also been used by some researchers in their studies, albeit infrequently. This procedure refers to the evaluation of the individual's creativity by a select group of experts. The study conducted by MacKinnon (1982) with architects illustrates this kind of evaluation; he requested experts in architecture to indicate the most creative professionals. Fleith, Rodrigues, Viana, and Cerqueira (2000) also used this procedure to select musicians recognized as creative by experts (e.g., music critics and directors of music colleges).

Immediate supervisors and peers have also been asked to assess the individual's creativity, especially in studies conducted in the organizational environment. Some studies using this method were described by Hocevar and Bachelor (1989), as the one developed by Calvin Taylor and colleagues with scientists in a research laboratory. The supervisors were asked to evaluate the scientists on several traits, such as productivity, motivation, integrity, independence, flexibility, persistence, cooperation, and creation.

Creativity in Products

Another approach to identify creativity has been the judgment of products. This approach involves judges who use predetermined criteria to assess the degree of creativity of a product. Amabile (1983, 1996b) is a scholar who has advocated the use of this modality of measurement. She conducted a series of studies in which an analysis of the product was undertaken with the purpose of quantifying the extent to which the product was creative. In these studies, a number of dimensions to be used in the evaluation of the product, with a descriptive definition of each of them, were provided to the judges. According to Amabile, high levels of reliability were observed among the judgments made.

In using this procedure, Amabile (1983) also considered it important that some requirements be met, such as the following: judges should be chosen among individuals who have familiarity in the domain, although the level of familiarity may vary from judge to judge; judges should share creativity criteria to a reasonable degree; judges should make their assessment independently of one another; and judges should rate the products in relation to one another on the dimensions in question, rather than evaluating them considering some absolute standards for the products in their domain. Furthermore, each judge should rate the products in a different random order and each judge should consider the various dimensions in question in a different random order. She also stated that the most important criterion for this assessment procedure is that the rating be reliable.

Technical Issues Related to Measures of Creativity

The growing interest in the study of creativity in recent decades has contributed significantly to the development of new inventories, checklists, and psychological tests. Different instruments to measure the various facets of creativity were constructed and have been used by researchers, psychologists, and other professionals from various areas. However, the tests of divergent thinking are the instruments most frequently used both in educational and psychological research (Cramond, 1999; Johnson & Fishkin, 1999; Michael & Wright, 1989). On the other hand, an analysis of the progress of research in respect to the evaluation of this construct in recent years, comparing, for example, the somewhat more recent literature (Cramond, 1999; Johnson & Fishkin, 1999; Piirto, 1999; Treffinger, 2003) with publications from earlier decades, such as Crockenberg's (1972) and Petrosko's (1978) articles, indicates that many issues still persist, with many fundamental problems unsolved.

Some of these problems are due to the fact that the proliferation of research on creativity and measurement instruments was not accompanied by significant advances in the theoretical foundation or in the organization of a systematic body of empirical knowledge, as previously pointed out by Greeno (1989). The author explained that the research in relation to creative thinking has made little progress compared with the rapid progress observed in the study of the cognitive structures. Moreover, the lack of consensus on the definition of creativity and the multidimensional character of the phenomenon limit the development of measuring instruments for the construct.

Still, in relation to tests of creativity, Treffinger (1987) highlighted that, in spite of the large number of tests that claim to be measures of creativity, they differ in many respects, once they mirror beliefs and preconceptions of their authors with regard to the nature of creativity. Treffinger

(1987) went further and pointed out that "unfortunately, the theoretical basis of such tests is often not sufficient to allow systematic tests of differential predictions" (p. 105).

Numerous authors also examined data on reliability and validity of different creativity assessment instruments, such as Anastasi (1988), Cropley (2005), Johnson and Fishkin (1999), Michael and Wright (1989), Tannenbaum (1983), and Treffinger (1987, 2003), pointing out inconsistent results in the studies carried out and difficulties in the selection of criteria (e.g., choice of external indicators of creative behaviors), which highlights the need for greater attention to the issue of measurement by those who investigate creativity. Several aspects have also been examined with respect to reliability and validity, as described in the next sections. However, it should be noted that throughout an analysis of the literature, the instruments most focused on are the tests of creative thinking, with a smaller number of references to other types of creativity measures.

Reliability

Three different forms of estimating reliability have been discussed in relation to the various measures of creativity, especially the tests of divergent thinking: the test-retest approach, through the correlation between the same form of a test administered at different times (stability or reliability over time); administering parallel or alternative forms of the same instrument (reliability of various forms of an assessment instrument); and the internal consistency approach, to estimate the reliability of the various items of a test within themselves. However, according to Michael and Wright (1989), depending on the type of measure of creativity, one or another approach would be more appropriate. In the case of measures of divergent thinking, for example, the use of alternative forms would be more appropriate, although in any kind of assessment that involves observation which occurs, for example, when using judges to evaluate the creativity of products, the internal consistency approach would be more appropriate.

As previously highlighted by Fleith and Alencar (1992), the reliability of the measures of creativity may be affected mainly by the heterogeneity of the sample domain (i.e., the absence of a clearly defined universe on creativity from which the items of the instruments are withdrawn). Other factors that may affect reliability are the sampling of content, the subjectivity of the evaluator, and motivational factors (both of the evaluator and of the evaluated).

Some of the difficulties encountered with reliability are due to the results of several studies with creative people that suggest substantial variations in their production in different periods. Also, motivational factors as well as context factors may affect the individual's performance on a test, and this will naturally reflect in some reliability indices of the measures. Moreover, problems have also been observed with regard to inter-rater reliability for measures of creativity when judges' evaluation is used. This is due to subjective factors such as the halo effect, which may influence the judgments made by the evaluator (Johnson & Fishkin, 1999).

Despite the factors that may influence the magnitude of reliability coefficients described previously, in the case of the Torrance Tests of Creative Thinking, several studies presented in the test manual (Torrance, 1966, 1974) indicate test–retest reliability coefficients above .50 for different measures. In one study described in the manual with a sample of higher education students, for example, Torrance obtained coefficients ranging from .68 to .85 for the various tests of his battery at an interval of 3 months. The studies reviewed by Torrance also indicated reliability coefficients that were higher for adults than for children, and higher in the measures of fluency and flexibility of verbal tests. In a study conducted by Alencar (1974a), with a sample of 159 fourth- and fifth-grade students, the coefficients ranged from .01 to .56 for 12 measures of creativity of the Torrance Tests of Creative Thinking in an interval of 4 months, much lower than those coefficients presented in the literature. On the other hand, in a validation study conducted by Wechsler (2002) with the Torrance Tests in Brazil, levels of reliability of .70 were reported.

Validity

Several authors have examined some issues of creativity assessment related to validity. This is the most important psychometric quality of an assessment instrument and is anchored, according to Wolf (as cited in Michael & Wright, 1989) in three issues, namely: (a) what the test is supposed to be measuring, (b) what the score derived from the application of a test means, and (c) how the score of an individual in a measure relates to other observable individual data.

Regarding criterion validity, which includes both concurrent and predictive validity, the challenge has been the identification of relevant criteria measures that are fully adequate. Concurrent validity has often been identified by comparing test results with assessments made by teachers and peers, which, as noted earlier, might present problems. This fact probably helps explain the lower concurrent validity coefficients of measures of creativity compared to the coefficients observed in other areas, such as intelligence and performance (Johnson & Fishkin, 1999). On the other hand, with respect to predictive validity, especially in the case of the Torrance Battery, studies have shown significant correlations between test results obtained at a given time and creative activities by the same individuals after 5 years or more. This aspect was examined by Johnson and Fishkin (1999) and Treffinger (1987) for the Torrance Tests of Creative Thinking. These authors described studies in which significant positive correlations were observed between test scores and follow-up data on creative achievements involving periods ranging from 9 months to 22 years. In a recent study, Cramond, Matthews-Morgan, Bandalos, and Zuo (2005) also obtained evidence about the predictive validity of Torrance.

In respect to the criterion validity of the tests of creativity, Michael and Wright (1989) highlighted some factors that may affect the interpretation of a validity coefficient, sometimes adversely. These authors indicated, for example, the need for the creative behavior observer or evaluator to prevent against the use that he or she sometimes, consciously or unconsciously, makes of information obtained from previously administered tests when evaluating an individual's performance in some criterion measures. Furthermore, the degree of reliability, of the predictor but also especially of the criterion measure, is a potentially attenuating factor of the magnitude of the validity coefficient. In most circumstances, the reliability of the measurement criterion tends to be lower than that associated with the test. If the criterion variable or test variable is not stable and consistent, this will certainly affect the degree of correlation between the measures.

Regarding construct validity, it has been pointed out that one of the requirements for its establishment is the convergent validity, in other words, the demonstration that the selected measure of a given behavior is related to other measures of the same construct and of other variables on the criterion, which have a relationship with the construct. A second requirement refers to the discriminative validity, demonstrating that the selected measure is independent of variables from other theoretically distinct constructs (Michael & Wright, 1989). One aspect that has been discussed with respect to construct validity refers to the fact that, since creativity involves a complex set of interrelated constructs, one of the biggest

challenges lies in operationalizing the theoretical constructs that constitute the foundation of creative behavior.

Several evidences of construct validity have been pointed out for some
creativity instruments, especially for the Torrance Battery. However, much
more research is needed on the vast majority of assessment measures available in order to meet the required psychometrics quality standards.

In respect to content validity, one of the greatest challenges is to meet
the requirement that the instrument content effectively cover a represen-
tative sample of the domain in question. This challenge was highlighted by
Torrance (1974) in his test manual. Because a person can behave creatively
in an almost infinite number of ways, it would be much more difficult to
try to develop a comprehensive battery of tests of creative thinking that
would constitute a sample of any universe of creative thinking abilities.
Torrance did not believe that someone can specify the number and extent
of the tests needed to give a complete or even adequate assessment of any
person's creative potential.

This fact justifies the criticism usually made of tests of creativity that
they only assess a very limited range of abilities and, therefore, it is inappropriate to consider the performance on a test as a general indicator of
creativity. On the other hand, this is a problem that is observed frequently
in the literature, as it is common to label as tests of creativity some measures that are essentially measures of a few cognitive abilities traditionally
related to creative thinking, such as fluency, flexibility, and originality. The
same is true with respect to some instruments that intend to assess personality traits that seem to favor the expression of the creative potential. What
happens is that different researchers investigate quite different phenomena
depending on the measures selected by them.

In our view, the researcher must always be attentive to the fact that the
creativity construct is multidimensional and complex, and should not mis-
take creativity with what is being measured by the available instruments. As
pointed out by Hocevar and Bachelor (1989), divergent thinking abilities
as well as attitudes, interests, and personality characteristics may be considered correlates of creative behavior, rather than creativity itself. This aspect
is particularly important because the nature of the items or tasks included,
for example, in the tests of creative thinking, as in the Torrance Tests of
Creative Thinking, do not lead to creative responses of a high standard,
and there is still the issue of a time limit for each item or task (5 to 10 minutes depending on the task), which is a factor that cannot be overlooked,

because the number of responses is emphasized in the test instructions. Treffinger (2003) adopted a similar point of view, considering that

> No single instrument or analytical procedure can capture the complex and multidimensional nature of creativity effectively and comprehensively. Systematic efforts to understand the creativity require a well-planned approach to studying individuals or groups, including both qualitative and quantitative data. (p. 62)

Application Conditions

Regarding application conditions, Michael and Wright (1989) stated the need to control some factors, such as the following: (a) the time available for the examinee to answer questions or time allowed for observers to make their judgments, (b) the difficulty level of words and the mode of presentation of the instructions, and (c) factors that may distract the attention of the respondent, such as noise, inappropriate lighting, clarity of instructions and illustrations contained in the instrument, and the sequence and number of tests administered. Regarding this last aspect, it is observed, for example, that the completion of all the tasks of the verbal part of the Torrance Battery seems rather tiresome, not only for children but also for adults. This causes many individuals to give a number of responses far short of what they could, especially in the last tests.

Treffinger (1987) reviewed several studies on the effect of administration conditions and psychological climate in the performance on tests of creativity. These studies indicated that tests results are affected by the procedures used during the administration of the instruments. For this reason, it is indispensable that those responsible for testing be trained in order to ensure adequate and comparable conditions in all of the administrations. Also, Johnson and Fishkin (1999) analyzed the effects of the environment in which the tests of creative thinking are administered in the obtained scores. These authors observed that the level of motivation, persistence, confidence, and perceived relevance of the proposed tasks may influence the results obtained in tests.

Our experience has also shown that the researcher should take special care in the use of creativity tests when the administration is to groups and not to individuals. Especially in the case of the use of tests of creative thinking for children and adolescents, and for people from disadvantaged socioeconomic levels, the motivational factor significantly affects performance in the tests—and when they are group-administered, it's difficult to control this variable. Torrance himself, author of the most used test for the assessment of creative thinking, highlighted that the way in which his test is administered affects the results. Even the moment of the administration has an effect on performance; Torrance (1988) pointed out that students at the end of the semester, for example, did not succeed so well in this test, even after participating in a creativity training program and with high motivation.

Concluding Remarks

An analysis of the state of the art on creativity measures leads us, therefore, to conclude that we are still at a preliminary stage of knowledge on this topic, with much to be done in order to clarify the many issues regarding creativity measures. As pointed out by Petrosko (1978), the great challenge of measuring creativity lies in the paradox of trying to build a standardized way of capturing something that evades standardization.

Although there are many obstacles in the process of assessing creativity, some recommendations can be made—for example, the recommendation of combining the assessment measures of creativity with the adopted definition or theoretical model. Also important is the use of multiple sources of creativity assessment. Another aspect to consider is the identification of consistent indicators and standards of creativity from different sources of information. It is also relevant that any assessment of creativity may be affected by many variables, such as the time necessary to complete the tasks and a respondent's physical condition and motivation. Furthermore, before selecting the assessment instrument to be used, it is necessary to analyze all available information about the instrument, especially that related to the validity and reliability of the measurement, as well as the possible cultural, social, ethnic, or gender biases. Even when an administrator follows these recommendations closely, however, the fact remains that "whatever the process, attempts to assess creativity are full of challenges" (Starko, 1995, p. 323).

CHAPTER 2

OBSTACLES TO PERSONAL CREATIVITY INVENTORY

Eunice M. L. Soriano de Alencar

One of the most discussed topics in the literature of creativity is the circumstances that favor its development and expression in different contexts. Simonton (2006), for example, in an analysis of the research on creativity in different countries, found out that studies on creativity in the educational context have been focusing mainly on issues concerning the best methods to promote the development of creativity and to identify creative children and young people. Similarly, in studies related to organizational psychology, the central focus has been on the identification of and how to facilitate creativity in the workplace.

Moreover, in recent theoretical contributions, a combination of cognitive, conative, and environmental attributes have been identified as necessary for creativity expression (Lubart, 2007; Lubart & Guignard, 2004). Sternberg (2003; Sternberg & Lubart, 1996), for example, in his Investment Theory of Creativity, considered that creativity requires the confluence of six distinct and interrelated factors, pointed out as the necessary resources for creative expression. They are: intellectual skills, thinking styles, knowledge, personality, motivation, and the environmental context. Also Amabile's (1996b, 1999) Componential Model of Creativity includes three components necessary for creativity expression: domain relevant skills, creativity relevant processes, and motivation. The first component includes several elements related to the level of expertise in a domain, such as knowledge, technical abilities, and special talents. The second component includes cognitive styles, domain of strategies that favor the production of new ideas, work style, and personality characteristics, such as persistence, independence, and risk taking. The third component is task motivation, which may be primarily intrinsic or extrinsic. According to Amabile, it is intrinsic motivation, the motivation to engage in some activity primarily for its own sake, which is conducive to creativity, although informational extrinsic motivation can also be conducive, particularly if it combines with high levels of intrinsic motivation. According to Amabile, all three components are strongly influenced by the social environment. Several factors in the environment can block creativity or foster it.

The factors that hinder individuals in taking advantage of their potential to create is a topic that has attracted the attention of several scholars devoted to the study of creativity. Some factors are eminently personal, such as personality characteristics that inhibit the production and implementation of new ideas (e.g., fear of appearing ridiculous, excessive desire for order and security, resistance to experimentation and risk-taking, and inflexibility). Other factors are of a sociocultural order, being directly linked to values and norms that contribute to hinder the expression of the potential to create. There are also factors in the work environment of organizations that may act as obstructions to the expression of individuals' creativity. Some of them are work overload, overemphasis on maintaining the status quo, excessive centralization of power, destructive competition, and inflexible organizational structure (Alencar, 2005; Amabile, 1995, 1999; Burnside, 1995).

Furthermore, practices that inhibit creativity in the educational context have been widely discussed by researchers, such as Alencar (2000a, 2002a, 2007), Craft (2005), MacKinnon (1978), Necka (1994), Sternberg and Lubart (1995), and, Tolliver (1985), among many others. These authors refer to different pedagogical practices that hinder the individual's creative development and expression, contributing to the strengthening of emotional and intellectual attributes that undermine the ability to create. Examples of such practices are:

- exaggerated emphasis on reproduction and memorization of knowledge;
- the use of exercises that require only one answer, cultivating too much fear of error and failure;
- greater emphasis on the students' incompetence, ignorance, and lack of ability, rather than the students' strengths;
- focusing solely on knowledge of the outside world, with little contribution to self-knowledge;
- development of a very limited number of cognitive abilities;
- focusing on the cultivation of obedience, passivity, dependence, and conformism;
- disregard for imagination and fantasy as important dimensions of the mind;
- use of strategies that prevent students from taking responsibility for their own learning and decision making, prioritizing the role of students as followers of instructions and information receivers;
- authoritarian management of the classroom;
- standardization of content; and
- insensitivity to individual differences.

Alencar (2007) also pointed out that a factor that inhibits creativity in educational institutions is the institutional culture prevalent in many schools, characterized by pressure on teachers who seek to introduce innovation in their teaching practices, making it difficult or even impossible for them to implement creative teaching. This pressure is, at times, voiced by peers or school administrators, who dictate how teachers should proceed in the classroom, with emphasis on uniformity of behavior. Conformism causes teachers to accommodate to the school routine, diminishing their enthusiasm for creative teaching practices. In this sense, Necka (1994) points out that institutions have their own history, culture, and customs, which are frequently characterized as convergent and anticreative.

With respect to obstacles to personal creativity, several authors, such as Adams (1986), Alamshah (1972), Alencar (1995a, 1995b; Alencar & Fleith, 2003a), Parnes (1967), Rickards and Jones (1991; Jones, 1993), Shallcross (1981), and VanDemark (1991), addressed this issue, referring to different factors that inhibit creativity and classifying them in different ways. Some authors include perceptual, cultural, emotional, and intellectual barriers in their taxonomies (Adams, 1986; Alencar, 1995b; Alencar & Fleith, 2003a) or historical, biological, sociological, and psychological barriers (Shallcross, 1981). Others differentiate between internal and external barriers (Parnes, 1967). Rickards and Jones (1991; Jones, 1993) have described strategic barriers, which refer to different approaches to solving problems; values, which includes personal beliefs and values that restrict the range of ideas covered; perceptual blockages; and self-image related to a lack of confidence in the value of their own ideas.

On the other hand, some authors, such as Arieti (1976) and Schwartz (1992), focused particularly on the sociodynamic factors of creativity that may facilitate or block the creative process, pointing to adverse forces to creativity present in Western society. These authors highlight that creativity is not haphazard, but rather is heavily influenced by environmental factors. They also consider the moments of creation as a result of complex social circumstances that cannot be ignored by those interested in learning more about the factors that positively or negatively influence creativity. Cropley (1997, 2005) also described the role of the social factors, such as norms and pressure to conform, that inhibit creativity. He calls attention, for example, to the rules children learn early in life that prevent them from taking certain courses of action (e.g., questioning conventional views, exposing themselves to the possibility of being wrong). The degree of openness in a society is also discussed by Cropley. According to him, people who produce something new in environments that are resistant to new ideas are likely to suffer various types of sanction.

Despite the vast literature about elements that can block the expression of creativity, empirical studies on this topic are greatly restricted to obstacles to creativity in the workplace, with several available instruments to identify these factors in this environment. One of these instruments was designed by Amabile and Gryskiewicz (1989) and includes scales to assess factors that would be stimulants to creativity and others that would be obstacles to creativity in the work environment. Another instrument that identifies barriers to individual creativity in organizational environments was developed by Rickards and Jones (1991; Jones, 1993). This instrument, named the Jones Inventory of Barriers, aims at identifying different types of obstacles that affect the expression of creativity in the workplace, such as perceptual blockages, values, and self-image.

An analysis of assessment instruments developed in the United States and European countries to identify organizational conditions that may stimulate or inhibit creativity was recently undertaken by Mathisen and Einarsen (2004). These authors noted greater emphasis on promoting factors than on those that prevent the expression of workplace creativity in all analyzed instruments. This was pointed out as a drawback because, according to them, a greater number of items related to impediments would improve the quality of the instruments examined.

In Brazil, Bruno-Faria and Alencar (1996) investigated stimuli and barriers to creativity in the workplace, after designing an instrument to identify facilitators and inhibiting features to creativity in the organizational context (Bruno-Faria & Alencar, 1998). This instrument, named Indicators of Climate for Creativity (ICC), similar to the one developed by Amabile and Gryskiewicz, includes a set of factors that represent stimulants to creativity in the workplace, such as an adequate physical environment, incentive to new ideas, freedom of action, and adequate salaries and benefits. It also encompasses factors that may be impediments to creativity in the workplace, such as an excessive number of tasks and scarcity of time, blockage to new ideas, and organizational problems (see a description of this instrument in Chapter 6).

There is, however, a scarcity of instruments to identify personal barriers to creativity. This was one of the reasons why we designed the Obstacles to Personal Creativity Inventory (Alencar, 1999).

Obstacles to Personal Creativity Inventory: Characteristics and Stages of its Construction

The starting point for the construction of the Obstacles to Personal Creativity Inventory was the development of several studies (Alencar, Fleith, & Virgolim, 1995; Alencar & Martínez, 1998; Alencar, Oliveira, Ribeiro, & Brandão, 1996), in which subjects were requested to complete, as truthfully as possible, the following sentence: "I would be more creative if . . ." This sentence was devised by the author based on a proposed exercise by Necka (1992) to identify internal barriers to the expression of the personal capacity to create. A content analysis of the responses indicated different categories of obstacles, including emotional, sociocultural, motivational/personality, and intellectual.

Some examples of responses obtained in these studies are presented below. Respondents indicate that they would be more creative if:

- I cultivated serenity more, leaving aside insecurity and the fear of facing the unknown.
- I had no fear of others' opinions. The fear of ridicule or of making mistakes makes me tremble and I cannot think of anything.
- I could send away the dragon of fear, of destructive criticism.
- I were not so afraid of making mistakes and failing.
- I had had more opportunities during my childhood.
- the society and the school where I studied had not cut my creativity short.
- I had more opportunities to explore my imaginative potential.
- I had courage, motivation, and freedom.
- I were not so lazy to think and to look for ideas to put them into practice.
- I had more knowledge.
- I had more time to develop my ideas.
- I were less criticized or I were not afraid of being criticized.

Based on the participants' responses obtained in these previous studies and in the literature on obstacles to the expression of creativity, a first version of the inventory to identify obstacles to the expression of personal creativity was constructed. It included 84 items related to the different categories of obstacles to personal creativity. These items were submitted to a semantic evaluation to ensure their understanding and to avoid ambiguous or poorly-developed items. For this evaluation, 15 high school students listened individually to the items and were requested to repeat the content of each one of them in their own words. They were also requested to evaluate the content of the items and the instrument as a whole. Fourteen items were then eliminated for being very similar in content to other items of the instrument or due to the respondents' difficulty in completely understanding the content of the items. Furthermore, five items were revised for lack of clarity in their wording.

The instrument was named Obstacles to Personal Creativity Inventory and administered to 389 university students from different courses (architecture, biology, chemistry, engineering, literature, medicine, pedagogy, physical education, political sciences, psychology, and statistics) in order to obtain data for the statistical validation. Each item is answered on a 5-point scale ranging from (1) strongly disagree to (5) strongly agree.

Data were analyzed using Statistical Package for the Social Sciences (SPSS) software. Initially, an exploratory analysis of the data was conducted to verify the normality of the distributions and the assumptions of factor analysis. Evidence of construct validity was obtained through an exploratory factor analysis with the principal component extraction option. An oblique rotation was performed. The criteria for retention of a factor were: (a) eigenvalue equal to or greater than 2.0; (b) factorial loading of the items equal to or higher than .30; and (c) a semantically interpretable factor. The alpha internal-consistency reliability coefficient was calculated for the four derived factors. All of them presented an alpha internal coefficient equal to or greater than .85. The number of items was reduced from 70 to 66 through the statistical analysis. However, a few items were included in more than one factor. These were variables that correlated with more than one factor and are called complex variables (Tabachnick & Fidell, 1996). The Obstacles to Personal Creativity Inventory is presented in Appendix A.

The four factors (modalities of obstacles) resulted from the analysis are presented below.

Factor 1–Inhibition/Shyness

Factor 1, labeled Inhibition/Shyness, includes 23 items especially concerning elements of an emotional nature that block the expression of personal creativity. The eigenvalue of this factor was 15.71, explaining 22.40% of the total variance and 60.87% of the common variance. The alpha internal-consistency coefficient was .91. The items of this factor, together with their factor loadings, are presented in Table 1.

Factor 2–Lack of Time/Opportunity

This factor includes 14 items that relate specially to the limited availability of time, resources, and opportunities to express the potential to create. The eigenvalue of this factor was 4.42, which explains 6.30% of the total variance and 17.12% of the common variance. The alpha internal-consistency coefficient was .85. The items of this factor, together with their factor loadings, are presented in Table 2.

TABLE 1

Factor Loadings of the Items Comprising Factor 1 (Inhibition/Shyness)

Item	Content	Factor loading
2	I were less shy to express my ideas.	.71
21	I were not afraid of expressing what I think.	.69
3	I were more spontaneous.	.64
8	I were more courageous.	.61
5	I were not so insecure.	.61
26	I were more extrovert.	.60
25	I were not afraid of carrying out my ideas.	.59
9	I had more initiative.	.54
20	I were not afraid of facing criticism.	.53
1	I believed more in myself.	.51
7	I were not afraid of making mistakes.	.49
6	I were more inclined to take risks.	.48
36	I were not afraid of what other people would think about me.	.47
30	I were not afraid of being misunderstood.	.46
10	I were not afraid of going against other people's ideas.	.44
29	I took better advantages of the opportunities to exercise my creativity.	.41
24	I expressed my ideas better.	.40
28	I did not have inferiority feelings in relation to others.	.39
49	I valued my ideas more.	.35
16	I were not afraid of facing the unknown.	.34
4	I were not so critical about myself.	.34
56	I were less fearful of ridicule.	.35
23	I let loose my imagination.	.31

TABLE 2

Factor Loadings of the Items Comprising Factor 2
(Lack of Time/Opportunity)

Item	Content	Factor loading
34	I had more opportunities to put my ideas into practice.	.63
31	I had more time to elaborate my ideas.	.56
15	I had more time.	.55
41	I had more resources (equipments, books, money, etc.) to put my ideas into practice.	.54
37	I had more opportunities to explore my potential.	.54
48	There were more cooperation among people.	.48
53	People valued new ideas more.	.48
35	I had more incentive from my colleagues.	.46
18	There were more recognition of the creative work.	.45
22	I had been more motivated by my teachers.	.44
40	I had more freedom to express what I think.	.40
46	My ideas were more valued.	.39
54	There were more respect regarding the differences among people.	.34
29	I took better advantage of the opportunities to exercise my creativity.	.31

Factor 3–Social Repression

The third factor, labeled Social Repression, includes 14 items concerning different factors of a social nature that block creativity. The eigenvalue of this factor was 3.58, which explains 5.1% of the total variance and 13.86% of the common variance. The alpha internal-consistency coefficient was .85. The items of this factor, together with their factor loadings, are presented in Table 3.

TABLE 3

Factor Loadings of the Items Comprising Factor 3 (Social Repression)

Item	Content	Factor loading
38	I had not had a strict upbringing.	.58
43	I had had more opportunities to make mistakes without being labeled an idiot.	.57
32	I had not been cut short by my family.	.53
42	I had not been trimmed by my teachers.	.50
44	I were less criticized.	.49
56	I were less fearful of ridicule.	.48
55	I were less bossy.	.43
52	There were more acceptance of fantasy where I live.	.39
36	I were not afraid of what other people would think about me.	.39
57	I were not so critical in relation to other peoples' ideas.	.37
27	I were less perfectionist.	.34
47	I ignored the criticism about my ideas.	.33
50	There were less competition among people.	.33
51	I were more encouraged to speak my mind.	.30

Factor 4–Lack of Motivation

The fourth factor, named Lack of Motivation, includes 20 items that relate mainly to the absence of personal motivation elements that facilitate the expression of creativity. The eigenvalue of this factor was 2.13, which explains 3.01% of the total variance and 8.15% of the common variance. The alpha internal-consistency coefficient was .88. The items of this factor, together with their factor loadings, are presented in Table 4.

TABLE 4

Factor Loadings of the Items Comprising Factor 4 (Lack of Motivation)

Item	Content	Factor loading
65	I were more enthusiastic.	-.68
63	I concentrated more on the tasks I do.	-.60
64	I were more curious.	-.57
12	I were less lazy.	-.54
58	I were more dedicated to what I do.	-.53
59	I had more energy.	-.53
45	I were more persistent.	-.53
11	I were not so laid back.	-.48
66	I were more knowledgeable.	-.46
62	I had more ideas.	-.44
17	I were a better observer.	-.44
61	I were less dependent of other people.	-.42
14	I were more organized.	-.39
13	I had more motivation to create.	-.37
19	I exercised more the habit of searching for new ideas.	-.37
60	I had more sense of humor.	-.36
23	I let loose my imagination.	-.34
39	I had more opportunities to access information.	-.33
33	I were more intelligent.	-.31
9	I had more initiative.	-.31

Studies Conducted with the Obstacles to Personal Creativity Inventory

Several studies were conducted with the Obstacles to Personal Creativity Inventory. The first one (Alencar, 2001b) was designed to investigate personal obstacles to creativity among university students. It also aimed to examine differences among male and female and private and public university students in their personal obstacles. The Obstacles to Personal Creativity Inventory was administered to 385 students from two universities, one private and one public. The results indicated that the highest mean was observed in the factor Lack of Time/Opportunity, and the lowest one in the Social Repression factor. Female students more significantly referred to items from the factor labeled Social Repression as inhibitors to their personal creativity, while male students referred to the cluster of obstacles labeled Lack of Motivation. Students from the private university presented highest means in all clusters of obstacles, compared to those from the public university, with these differences being statistically significant in two of them, Inhibition/Shyness and Lack of Time/Opportunity.

A second study (Alencar, Fleith, & Martínez, 2003) compared Brazilian and Mexican college students (N = 540) in the different clusters of obstacles, besides examining differences between gender. Mexican students obtained higher scores compared to Brazilian students in the factor Lack of Motivation. On the other hand, differences among male and female students were observed in the cluster of obstacles named Inhibition/Shyness, with significantly higher mean by the female students. Lack of Time/Opportunity was the most frequent cluster of obstacles and Social Repression the least frequent.

The obstacles to personal creativity were also investigated in a sample of 544 elementary to higher education teachers (Alencar & Fleith, 2003a). Similarly to the results of the previous studies, Lack of Time/Opportunity was the cluster of obstacles with the highest mean, while the lowest mean was in Social Repression. Moreover, differences were observed among teachers from different educational levels. First- to fourth-grade elementary school teachers, who were predominantly female, presented significantly higher means in the Inhibition/Shyness and Social Repression factors, compared with teachers from other levels of education. The female teachers' mean was significantly higher in the Social Repression factor.

Similar results to those obtained in the studies described above, with respect to the cluster of obstacles more frequently and less frequently pointed out, were observed by Joly and Guerra (2004) in a study with 121 university students, by Castro (2007) in a sample of 53 fourth-grade teachers, and Ribeiro and Fleith (2007) in a sample of 82 university teachers. Joly and Guerra also observed differences among students from different courses in two clusters of obstacles. Psychology students, compared to pharmacy and business administration students, presented higher means in Inhibition/Shyness, while pharmacy students, compared to those from the computer science course, presented higher means in the factor Lack of Motivation. On the other hand, Castro did not identify differences in the several clusters of obstacles between teachers from public and private schools and with greater or lesser teaching experience.

Data on the concurrent validity of the Obstacles to Personal Creativity Inventory were obtained in a study conducted by Alencar et al. (2003) with 64 engineering students. The different clusters of obstacles evaluated by the inventory were presented to these students during a semistructured interview that aimed at exploring the factors that, according to them, contribute more to the expression of personal creativity as well as those taken as more inhibiting to the expression of the capacity to create, in university students as well as in professionals of the work market. Possible differences between gender and between students and professionals with regard to the frequency of the different clusters of obstacles were also explored during the interview. Similar results to those obtained in previous studies with the Obstacles to Personal Creativity Inventory were found. Social Repression was pointed out as the least frequent obstacle and Lack of Time/Opportunity as the most frequent among students and professionals. According to the participants of the study, the cluster of obstacles named Social Repression was more frequent among women and Lack of Motivation more frequent among men.

It is noteworthy that Lack of Time and Opportunity was the factor more frequently pointed out as an obstacle to the expression of the personal creativity in all studies conducted previously. Items that illustrate this factor are: I would be more creative if (a) I had more opportunities to put my ideas into practice, (b) I had more time to elaborate my ideas, (c) there were more recognition of creative work, and (d) I had more opportunities to explore my potential.

The content of the majority of this factor's items refers to conditions external to the individual, including sociocultural elements that prevent the individual from using his or her creative potential to a greater degree. In previous studies, such as those conducted by Amabile and Gryskiewicz (1989), Bruno-Faria and Alencar (1996, 1998), and Talbot (1993) of employees from different types of organizations, scarcity of time was pointed out as a frequent inhibitor to the expression of creativity. Moreover, several authors, such as Arieti (1976), Amabile (1996b), Montuori and Purser (1995), and Lubart (1999, 2007), pointed out sociocultural variables that might restrict or promote creativity. Arieti (1976), for example, highlighted that to promote a climate for creativity, society must present some characteristics, one of them being the access to means that enable the individual to express his or her creativity in specific areas, calling attention to the importance of encouragement and incentive to the expression of creativity. Also Lubart (1999) examined the cultural influences on the manifestation of creativity, highlighting factors that restrict it, such as lack of opportunity.

Concluding Remarks

There is a growing recognition of the importance of creativity for the individual, organizations, and society. It has been regarded as a valuable resource that helps the individual to take greater benefit from opportunities, to respond in a more productive way to challenges in his or her personal and professional life, and to cope better with unexpected situations. However, despite this recognition, misconceptions about creativity are still very frequent. The idea of creativity as an eminently individual and intrapsychic phenomenon, for example, prevails in many countries, as well as the idea that the creative expression would occur independently of the environmental conditions. The conception of creativity as a natural talent present in only a few individuals is also frequent. Many people also ignore that every person is naturally creative and that the extent to which creativity blossoms depends largely on the environmental incentive and support. Furthermore, it is common to ignore that the capacity to create might be expanded through the strengthening of attitudes, values, beliefs, and other personal attributes that predispose the person to think in an independent, flexible, and imaginative way. Moreover, many ignore that creativity is not something that happens by chance, but might be deliberately employed, managed, and developed.

In spite of the importance of creativity, there is a scarcity of empirical studies about possible factors that inhibit or block its expression at the personal level. According to Jones (1993), the reasons that might help explain the scarcity of studies in respect to obstacles to creativity are:

The topic is complex and does not lend itself to quick answers; the variables need to be viewed interactively, rather than in isolation; similarities and differences in concepts and definitions have not been carefully examined; effective methods of assessment have not been developed; collaboration on the topic has been limited (p. 183).

The instrument described in this chapter contributes to this direction. It can be useful for diagnostic purposes as well as in training and personal development programs. It is known that the identification of barriers to personal creativity constitutes the first step in the process of promoting the necessary conditions for overcoming them. This identification allows for the organization of intervention strategies, which might help individuals to be less susceptible to obstacles that prevent them from using their ability to create.

However, the Obstacles to Personal Creativity Inventory requires further studies to strengthen its psychometric properties. With this purpose, it is suggested that research be carried out to complement the data obtained with this tool with other data collected through interviews and/or observations of individuals in different natural or experimental situations or with the use of other measures, such as personality tests. This would contribute to the concurrent and discriminative validity of the inventory. It is also recommended to investigate the test-retest reliability in the short and long term, applying this instrument to the same individuals in follow-up administrations.

It should also be pointed out that many of the barriers that may be identified through the use of the Obstacles to Personal Creativity Inventory reflect practices in the family and/or at school, which dwarfs the possibilities of the use by the individual of his or her creativity. It's relevant that socializing agents are attentive to promote environments in which creativity is more likely to flourish. It is also necessary to help individuals to be less susceptible to obstacles that block their creativity. This would contribute to reduce the loss of creative talent that results from an environment that restricts the emergence and development of creativity.

CHAPTER 3

ASSESSMENT OF THE CLIMATE FOR CREATIVITY IN THE CLASSROOM

Denise de Souza Fleith

T he concept of creativity as a multifaceted phenomenon has gained momentum especially since the last decades of the 20th century. From this perspective, individual factors and environmental variables would be in dynamic interaction, interfering in the creative process. Csikszentmihalyi explained (1996):

> To understand creativity it is not enough to study the individuals who seem most responsible for a novel idea or a new thing. Their contribution, while necessary and important, is only one link in a chain, a phase in a process. (p. 7)

Csikszentmihalyi (1996) added that:

> An idea or product that deserves the label "creative" arises from the synergy of many sources and not only

from the mind of single person. It is easier to enhance creativity by changing conditions in the environment than trying to make people think more creatively. (p. 1)

The environment, therefore, plays a key role in stimulating the creative potential, and the study of its influence on creative output cannot be neglected. One of the most investigated environments in creativity research is the school (Fleith, 2011; Simonton, 2006). According to Amabile (1996b), "of all the social and environmental factors that might influence creativity, most can be found in some form in the classroom" (p. 203).

The studies on creativity in the school environment have focused on personological characteristics associated with creativity (Martínez, 2006), favorable and inhibiting pedagogical practices to the creative potential (Alencar, 2000b; Alencar & Fleith, 2007), the perception of students and teachers about the classroom climate for creativity (Alencar & Fleith, 2004b; Fleith, 2000; Fleith & Alencar, 2006; Ribeiro & Fleith, 2007), and the creativity assessment of students from different school types and levels of education (Castro, 2007; Gontijo, 2007; Matos & Fleith, 2006). Moreover, little has been invested in the construction and validation of creativity measures, especially in Brazil.

The purpose of this chapter is, therefore, to present a scale for assessing the classroom climate for creativity, explaining its conception, construction, and validation. This chapter is divided into four sections. Initially, we analyzed characteristics of the classroom climate conducive to creativity, including the presentation of research results. The second section will focus on the process of designing the scale and the third will explain how the instrument has been validated, including results of studies on which that scale was used. Closing remarks will be made in the final section, highlighting the implications of using the scale and the limitations of the instrument. The instrument itself can be found in Appendix B: Classroom Climate for Creativity Scale.

Characteristics of the Classroom Climate Favorable to Creativity

There are many reasons to invest in the development of creative potential. According to Alencar (2002b), creativity is an ability that must be encouraged in an educational context because it promotes well-being as a result of emotional experiences of creative learning, contributing to a better quality of life. Moreover, this ability contributes to professional trainings, because creativity is presented as a critical tool that helps an individual to cope with the adversities and challenges of our time.

A reason also mentioned by Csikszentmihalyi (2006) is the rapid globalization of economic and social systems that apparently would lead to a better distribution of labor and resources and a better integration of beliefs, values, and knowledge. However, that globalization could also generate a greater division between rich and poor as well as the predominance of values of more powerful economic cultures. Another reason given by the author is that the specialization of knowledge could lead to its fragmentation. According to Csikszentmihalyi (2006), the great science discoveries in the last century were the products generated at the interface of disciplines. Addressing these challenges requires the ability to recognize emerging realities, understand their implications, and formulate responses that will generate new ideas and products. "And that requires creativity" (Csikszentmihalyi, 2006, p. xix). And how can schools prepare students for this creative task?

Aiming to develop creativity in schools, Sternberg (2000) suggested the following strategies: (a) to allocate time for creative thinking, (b) to reward creative ideas and products, (c) to encourage students to take risks; (d) to accept mistakes as part of the learning process, (e) to allow the students to imagine other points of view, (f) to provide opportunities for students to explore the environment and to question assumptions, (g) to identify interests, (h) to formulate problems, (i) to generate multiple hypotheses, and (j) to focus on general ideas rather than specific facts.

Amabile (1989) also proposed alternatives of creating a classroom climate conducive to creativity. She highlighted, for example, that teachers should provide constructive and meaningful feedback, emphasizing cooperation rather than competition, and involve students in evaluating their learning process. Amabile also suggested that students should have choices and learning experiences close to real life; share their interests, experiences, ideas, and materials in the classroom; and have opportunities to evaluate their own work. The author also noted that the school must provide a learning environment that is perceived as important and fun as well as a classroom that contains diverse and abundant material.

In a study conducted by Fleith (2000), both teachers and students in third and fourth grade characterized the context of the classroom that fosters creativity as one that offers the opportunity for choices, accepts different ideas, and focuses on student's interests. On the other hand, the environment that inhibits creativity would be the one in which ideas are ignored, teachers are controllers, and the educational structure is excessive.

Csikszentmihalyi (2006) drew further attention to the discrepancy between what students need and what the school offers. This author believes that schools teach students to answer, but not to question. Moreover, the contents are discussed in isolation, complicating the integration of several disciplines. Csikszentmihalyi highlighted that young people must learn how to relate and apply past ways of knowledge acquiring and processing into a constantly changing kaleidoscope of ideas and events. According to the author, injecting creativity into the educational system is needed to help students find out what they really love as well as to help immerse them into that domain. Likewise, he suggested that teachers should be selected based on their interest in teaching and that the pedagogical method should privilege the imagination and involvement of students in the learning process.

Research conducted by Alencar (1997b) and Alencar, Collares, Dias, and Julião (1993) indicated that, according to both high school and university students' perception, creativity is not encouraged by teachers. Alencar and Fleith (2004b) also investigated the perceptions of professors and students in relation to the occurrence of practices that contribute to the development of creativity in universities. The results revealed that teachers, when compared to their students, have a more favorable perception of the practices that contribute to the development of creative potential. Similar results were obtained by Silva (2000), by comparing the views of students and high school teachers regarding the creative characteristics of teachers and types of classes. The teachers described themselves as dynamic and motivating, while the students perceived them as boring.

Based on the results of their research, Alencar (2000b) and Fleith (2002) characterized a classroom climate conducive to creativity as the one that:

- protects the student's creative work from destructive criticism;
- leads the students to become aware of their talents, strengthening their self-esteem;
- develops the students' ability to think in terms of exploring consequences, suggesting modifications, and improving their own ideas;
- encourages students to reflect on what they'd like to know better;
- involves students in solving real-world problems;
- enables students to participate in a choice of problems or activities to be developed;
- encourages students to develop unique products;
- considers the students' cognitive, emotional and social characteristics and needs, their adjustment to school contexts, as well as the desired student profile in each type of school;
- implements activities that encourage students to generate many ideas;
- develops activities that would encourage students to explore consequences for events that could occur in the future;
- provides students with information that is important, interesting, contextualized, meaningful, and interconnected;
- provides an environment of a psychologically safe classroom in which students are not afraid to express themselves.

The responsibility of school in the development of creative abilities is unquestionable. Several strategies for stimulating the creative potential in school have been suggested, as shown earlier. The next step is to assess the extent to which these strategies are implemented. Therefore, identifying factors that favor or inhibit the creativity of individuals in the classroom becomes an important goal for the evaluation of schools as creativity promoters. In this sense, given the relevance of the topic and lack of instruments in the area, we designed and validated a scale of the classroom climate for creativity, which will be described below.

Designing the Classroom Climate
for Creativity Scale

The Classroom Climate for Creativity Scale has been based on a literature review. The theoretical framework that supported the instrument was the perspective of systems proposed by Csikszentmihalyi (1996, 1999), which conceives creativity as a result of the interaction of a system composed of three subsystems: person, domain, and field. Domain is defined as an organized body of knowledge associated with a given field. The contribution of the subsystem field for the stimulation of creativity is manifested as the knowledge is organized and information is easily accessible. Field, in turn, includes all persons who can affect the structure of the domain, such as teachers, judges, and institutions. Thus, it is important that the potential and interest of young people are recognized by a more experienced member of the field. The subsystem person includes the individual genetic background and personal experiences. Interest and curiosity can be stimulated through positive experiences and an environment that encourages creative expression (Fleith & Alencar, 2005). The approach proposed by Csikszentmihalyi (1994, 1996, 1999) argued that the environment can affect the production of something new as well as its acceptance, because creativity is considered a socially and culturally constructed phenomenon. In this sense, you should not just encourage people to think more creatively, you must create environmental conditions that favor creative production. The most important issue being investigated is, therefore, "Where's the creativity?" and not "What is creativity?".

Fifty-one items composed the first version of the scale. The instrument items were written in the affirmative in order to avoid any misunderstanding by young students as recommended by Gable and Wolf (1993). The items were answered in a 5-point scale: (1) never, (2) rarely, (3) sometimes, (4) often, and (5) always. All five points of the scale were written and plotted, gradually, using either a smiley or sad face (e.g., ☺ ☹).

Next, third- and fourth-grade teachers analyzed the items to ascertain whether the language used was clear and appropriate for students of this level of schooling. Thirteen items were retained, 13 were reworked, and 26 were deleted. The second version of the scale contained, then, 26 items. There was also a variation scale of frequency: The word "rarely" used in point (2) was later called "a few times."

Subsequently, we carried out a pilot study to semantically evaluate the items constructed in order to ensure students' understanding and to avoid ambiguity and inappropriate formulations. The instrument was administered to 80 third- and fourth-grade students from public schools and two private schools in Brazil. The scale items were read aloud to students. The instruction given to students was: "The sentences that you will read in this questionnaire are related to what happens in your classroom. You will indicate with an X on the face that best shows what happens in your classroom. Choose only one face for each phrase and be careful not leave any sentence without an answer." They were asked whether they had any questions concerning the procedures for answering the questions, the understanding of the items, and the meaning of words contained in the scale. A change was made with respect to the graphical representation of the scale. It was chosen to use only happy faces, but gradually increasing size points (☺ ☺ ☺), once it was noted that students avoided the sad face whether they agreed or disagreed with the content of the item.

Based on the results of the pilot study, nine items were revised and one item was discarded. This procedure resulted in 25 items that made up the instrument, which was then applied to a sample of 644 third- and fourth-grade students in order to obtain data to validate it (Fleith & Alencar, 2005).

Participants included 215 (33.4%) students from public schools and 428 (66.5%) from private schools. One student did not report the type of school he attended. Among the students, 346 (53.7%) were males and 297 (46.1%) females, 382 (59.3%) were in third grade and 260 students (40.4%) were in fourth. Two students did not indicate the grade in which they were enrolled. The average age of participants was 9.36 years, ranging from 7 to 13 years.

Validation of the Classroom Climate for Creativity Scale

In an attempt to investigate the construct validity of the scale, its internal structure was verified through factor analysis. A principal axis factor analysis, with varimax rotation, was used, preceded by exploratory data analysis to verify the normality of distributions and the assumptions of factor analysis. The KMO was .86 and Bartlett test of sphericity was significant. There have been no more than 2.15% of missing cases per variable. To check the reliability of generated factors, the coefficient alpha of internal consistency was used (Fleith & Alencar, 2005).

Initially, six factors were extracted based on the Kaiser criterion (Gable & Wolf, 1993), in which the *eigenvalue* of the factor should be equal to or greater than 1. However, one factor was dropped because it included only one item. This item was also dismissed because it was not allocated in any of the other factors. Only items with factor loading equal to or greater than .30 were considered. Two items were discarded because they were not allocated in any one of the factors. The solution of five factors explained 31% of the variance. Twenty-two items comprised the final version of the Classroom Climate for Creativity Scale (Fleith & Alencar, 2005).

Factor 1 was named Teacher's Support to the Student's Expression of Ideas and included five items related to the support that the teacher provides to students to express his or her opinion, creating a climate of respect for the ideas, and helping students to feel safe in expressing their ideas in the classroom (see Table 5). The alpha reliability coefficient for this factor was .73.

Factor 2 was named Student's Self-Perception of Creativity and included four items regarding students' self-image in relation to their level of creativity (see Table 6). Factor 3 was named Student's Interest in Learning because it includes six items related to students' involvement in schoolwork (see Table 7). The alpha coefficients for both factors were .66.

Factor 4 was named Student's Autonomy and includes four items that relate to a personality trait associated with creativity (see Table 8). The coefficient alpha reliability for this factor was .55. Factor 5, Teachers' Incentive to Student's Ideas Production, includes three items relating to attitude of acceptance and encouragement from the teacher to the ideas generated by students (see Table 9). The alpha reliability coefficient for this factor was .58.

TABLE 5

Factor Loadings of the Items Comprising Factor 1
(Teacher's Support to the Student's Expression of Ideas)

Item	Content	Load
1	The teacher pays attention to my ideas.	.73
12	The teacher cares about what I have to say.	.66
3	My ideas are welcome.	.50
7	The teacher gives me enough time to think about a story I have to write.	.47
2	I have a chance to participate in many activities.	.34

Note. Explained variance = 7.84. Reliability index = .73.

TABLE 6

Factor Loadings of the Items Comprising Factor 2
(Student's Self-Perception of Creativity)

Item	Content	Load
10	I have many ideas.	.59
6	I think I'm creative.	.58
8	I use my imagination.	.49
20	I am proud of myself.	.37

Note. Explained variance = 6.60. Reliability Index = .66.

TABLE 7

Factor Loadings of the Items Comprising Factor 3
(Student's Interest in Learning)

Item	Content	Load
13	I like the content taught.	.72
15	I learn about things that I really like.	.51
9	Work is fun.	.38
11	When I start a task, I like to finish it.	.36
18	I learn many things.	.32
22	I use books for research when I want to know more about a topic.	.30

Note. Explained variance = 6.59. Reliability index = .66.

TABLE 8

Factor Loadings of the Items Comprising Factor 4
(Student's Autonomy)

Item	Content	Load
16	I can make choices about what I want to do.	.59
17	I get so interested in my schoolwork that I do not know what is happening around me.	.43
4	I try to do things in different ways.	.40
5	The teacher asks me to show my work to other students.	.39

Note. Explained variance = 5.18. Reliability index = .55.

TABLE 9

Factor Loadings of Items Comprising Factor 5
(Teachers' Incentive to Student's Ideas Production)

Item	Content	Load
14	The teacher asks me to think of new ideas.	.61
21	The teacher asks me to think of many ideas.	.61
19	The teacher asks me to try when I do not know the answer to a question.	.36

Note. Explained variance = 5.67. Reliability Index = .58.

Studies Conducted With the Classroom Climate for Creativity Scale

Recent studies employing The Classroom Climate for Creativity Scale were conducted. In research by Fleith and Alencar (2006) with third- and fourth-grade students from public and private schools, for example, Factor 3 of the scale (Student's Interest for Learning) was the factor best assessed by the participants. On the other hand, Factor 4 (Student's Autonomy) had the lowest average. The results also indicated that female students had more positive perceptions when compared to males when it comes to Factor 1 (Teacher's Support to the Student's Expression of Ideas), Factor 3 (Student's Interest in Learning), and Factor 4 (Student's Autonomy). Moreover, fourth-grade students assessed Factors 1 and 4 more satisfactorily than third graders. Also, the students of private schools had more positive perceptions about Teacher's Support to the Student's Expression of Ideas (Factor 1) and student's self-perception with respect to creativity (Factor 2) than students from public schools.

Matos and Fleith (2006) also examined the perception of climate for creativity in the classroom of students from open, intermediary, and traditional schools. One hundred and seventy-four fourth-grade students from eight private schools participated in this study. Results indicated that there were no significant differences between students from open, intermediary, and traditional schools in relation to the five factors measured by the scale. The results also indicated that there were no significant differences between male and female students regarding the factors assessed by The Classroom Climate for Creativity Scale.

Another study, implemented by Fleith and Alencar (2008), investigated the relationship between creativity, self-concept, and perception of the classroom climate for creativity of fourth-grade students enrolled in public and private schools. The results revealed significant positive correlations between creativity, four dimensions of self-concept (Scholastic Competence, Social Acceptance, Physical Appearance, and Behavioral Conduct), and four factors of the climate of the classroom for creativity (Factor 2: Student's Self-Perception of Creativity, Factor 3: Student's Interest in Learning, Factor 4: Student's Autonomy, and Factor 5: Teachers' Incentive to Student's Ideas Production).

Castro (2007) examined the perception of the classroom climate for creativity of 967 fourth-grade students from teachers with more and less teaching experience. Students from more experienced teachers, compared to students of teachers with less teaching experience, felt that they were given more support from the teacher's expression of ideas (Factor 1) and that the atmosphere of the classroom stimulated interest in learning (Factor 3). Moreover, the results indicated that private school students perceived the climate of the classroom as more creative in favor of their autonomy (Factor 4) compared to public school students.

Final Considerations

The five factors measured by The Classroom Climate for Creativity Scale assess teachers' behaviors conducive to students' creative expression and student characteristics associated with creativity. It may be noted that the instrument items include individual and environmental aspects that are in line with the systemic perspective of creativity used in this work.

In terms of use, this scale can be employed for a diagnosis of the climate for creativity in the classroom, including the identification of factors that enable or inhibit the expression of creativity in third and fourth graders. Based on this diagnosis, strategies of intervention can be planned in order to promote favorable conditions for the development of the creative potential in the classroom. Thus, the instrument can help in guiding the teacher about what aspects of teaching and learning should be further encouraged in the classroom and what practices should be avoided, as well as an indication of what aspects of training teachers deserve to be reviewed in order to implement practices that foster creativity in the school context (Fleith & Alencar, 2005). This instrument can also be used to collect data for future research in the area of creativity and to evaluate the effectiveness of exercises and training programs implemented to stimulate creativity in the school context.

It is important to point out some limitations of the instrument. From a methodological point of view, reliability indices obtained for some of the factors of the scale are below the optimal level. According to Gable and Wolf (1993), a criterion of retaining factors, considering its reliability, is an alpha coefficient of internal consistency equal to or greater than .70. It is, therefore, our intention to improve the scale so as to increase the reliability indices of the factors measured by it. Moreover, from the studies, we observed that the use of the scale is more appropriate for students enrolled in fourth grade. Younger students (third graders) found more difficulty in understanding the items of the instrument and instructions for response.

Unquestionably, it is a great challenge to assess the extent to which classroom climate favors the development of creative expression and, based on this, propose and implement teaching practices that promote creativity. As Novaes (1992) explained, "between passively accepting the ready, the predetermined and the need to build, conquer and transform, there is a radical change in attitudes of people at a personal and social level" (p. 93). As a possible way to go forward, Novaes (1992) suggested that:

The concreteness of a creative education will come more as a result of experiences and commitments that arise in life and school routines than in efforts focused solely on certain situations or educational moments, triggered by this or that element alone. (Novaes, 1992, p. 99)

CHAPTER 4

INVENTORY OF TEACHING PRACTICES FOR CREATIVITY IN HIGHER EDUCATION

Eunice M. L. Soriano de Alencar
and Denise de Souza Fleith

There is an increasing recognition of the need to prepare students for the present scenario, where the ability to think and solve new problems occupies a central place. The rationale for this need is the rapid pace of change and unprecedented progress that characterize modern times, resulting in a significant part of the content taught in school becoming obsolete in a short period of time. In the complex world of work, a premium is placed on creativity, and the individual with the ability to think creatively, who demonstrates efficient strategies to solve unpredictable problems, is highly valued.

Therefore, initiatives have been taken by governments of different countries aiming at the discussion and implementation of educational policies that ensure the development of students' creative abilities (Cohen, 1997; Craft, 1998, 2006; Strom & Strom, 2002; Tan, 2001). Despite this recognition and government initiatives, flaws have been found regarding the promotion of creativity in different levels of education. According to several scholars, such as Alencar (1995a, 1995b, 2001a, 2002a), Cole, Sugioka, and Yamagata-Lynch (1999), Csikszentmihalyi (2006), Furman (1998), MacKinnon (1978), and Sternberg (1991), it is not rare for school to discourage the expression of creativity and even punish it. Regarding higher education, criticisms were made by Paulovich (1993) in the United States, Tolliver (1985) in Canada, Cropley (1997, 2005) in Germany, and Castanho (2000) and Rosas (1985) in Brazil because of the limited or lack of incentive for creativity.

Paulovich (1993), for example, criticized university education for not encouraging creative and independent thinking. According to the author, students who are anxious for good grades are forced to memorize and regurgitate an incredible volume of facts at a pace that prevents even the most enthusiastic of them to reflect on the material taught or be intellectually stimulated. Also Tolliver (1985) drew attention to a number of educational practices in Canadian higher education that inhibit the expression of creativity and punish the more creative students. He highlighted that, due to what commonly occurs in the university, "educators may be encouraging students to commit intellectual atrocities to survive" (p. 35).

Similarly in Germany, Cropley (1997) highlighted that schools and universities were producing a large number of graduates, but most of them were trained to simply apply the already known in a conventional manner. Cropley (2005) analyzed various studies conducted in different countries that found indifference and even hostility to creativity on the part of institutions of higher education. In one of the studies reviewed by Cropley, for example, it was found that engineering students from a North American university who preferred trying new solutions to the problems dropped out of a course three times more frequently than students who preferred conventional solutions. He also presented data collected in Australia that revealed that universities were not providing the necessary training, because three quarters of all new graduates were considered by employers as "deficient" in creativity, problem solving, and critical and independent thinking. Cropley emphasized the great necessity of an education that encourages creativity, signaling the beneficial effects of pedagogical strategies that nurture creativity on students' motivation, attitudes toward school, and self-image.

Moreover, Csikszentmihalyi (2006) stated that most common in higher education is the presence of curriculum proposals aimed solely at the transmission of knowledge, which is no longer enough in today's world. It's also necessary for students to be able to relate and apply this knowledge in a changing scenario of ideas and events, which requires creativity. He pointed out several challenges to higher education, as, for example, the tendency for increased specialization of knowledge, which makes it difficult for the student to have sight of the interfaces among disciplines, loosing a catalyst of fertilization of new ideas.

In Brazil, the scarcity of space for the development of creativity in university courses has been pointed out by several authors, such as Alencar (1995b, 1996, 1997b; Alencar & Fleith, 2004b), Castanho (2000), and Rosas (1985). Rosas stated, for example, that "it is in higher education where creativity is less discussed. With the exception of schools and/or departments of arts, it seems that teachers from other departments have much more to do than to worry about imagination, fantasy and creation" (p. 122). Similarly, Castanho (2000) considered that:

> We may affirm that our colleges are, in general, low or nothing creative. To develop creativity seems to be such a simple goal. However, creativity is one of the rarest characteristics found in most of our students, who have been educated to have conformist and homogeneous attitudes. (p. 77)

Alencar (2002a) also drew attention to the prevalence of a culture of learning in many schools which establishes limits far below the practically unlimited possibilities of the human potential to create. In several studies, Alencar (1994, 1995a, 1995c, 1997b) observed the practice of teachers of requiring mostly memorization and reproduction of knowledge and obsolete information from the students. This practice was found out, for example, in an analysis of the content of exam questions used by teachers from different subjects, who required only the reproduction of the content given in class or presented in the textbooks. At the higher education level, in a study on students' perceptions regarding the extent to which the expression of creativity was encouraged by their teachers, Alencar (1995c, 1997b) observed conditions that reflected low incentive for the development of the students' creative abilities. Furthermore, Alencar and Fleith (2004a) found, in a study with engineering students and engineers, that they mentioned emotional elements, such as shyness, insecurity, fear of expressing—as well as the conditions of the university and of the Engineering course—such as the prevailing teaching practices and the detachment of the university from the labor market, as factors that inhibit the expression and implementation of students' new ideas, as may be seen in Table 10.

On the other hand, Fleith (2000) highlighted that many teachers are aware of the characteristics that enhance students' creativity in the classroom. However, the transference to practice appears to be intuitive. The limited information on how to cultivate creative abilities in the classroom may be explained by the lack of formal creativity training in teacher education. As Novaes (1999) proclaimed:

> The development of creative abilities in humans is a priority in the university of the third millennium, since the automation in today's times has limited the ability to build a human world. (p. 15)

Although the previously mentioned authors have drawn attention to the need to promote better conditions for the development of creativity in university courses, there is a scarcity of empirical studies assessing the extent and frequency to which teaching behaviors promote the expression of creativity. There is also a lack of standardized instruments that aim at evaluating the extent to which teachers have been presenting behaviors and teaching practices that favor the development and expression of creative abilities of their students. The few inventories described in the literature, such as the ones used by Furman (1998) and Soh (2000), were not built specifically for the use of college students. The first was applied to teachers and elementary school students and validated in a second sample of only 117 teachers who taught in primary and secondary schools. This study was developed to fill this gap. It aimed at designing and validating an instrument that assesses students' perceptions of the extent to which their teachers were presenting behaviors and implementing teaching practices that promote the development and expression of their creativity. Two more versions of this instrument were also designed to be answered by university professors, being one of the versions in the final stages of validation.

TABLE 10

Responses of Engineering Students and Engineers About Factors That Inhibit the Expression/Implementation of Students' New Ideas

RESPONSES
Depending on how the teacher focuses on the class or work, it occasionally inhibits the person's ability to awaken his/her critical thinking and creativity. The student is withheld in that place; he cannot try to find another way of approaching that particular subject. It depends if the teacher gives the students freedom. (Engineering student)
In the classroom things are taught and we are obligated to sit down and only listen to the explanation, with no chance of doing anything different. (Engineering student)
Lack of time to create. In this case, the workload is heavy and the theoretical part is also very heavy. (Engineering student)
The university is very deficient. It does not invest in research with the students . . . Look at my case. I was there for hours on end. I had classes all day, 5 years, sitting down from eight to noon and from 1:30 p.m. to 5:30 p.m. every single day. We have practical classes only in the fourth and fifth year. We just sat staring at the blackboard, only seeing theory, theory, theory . . . Students are there, stuck in a chair all day, looking at a blackboard, listening to the teacher who always teaches in the same way every day, week, 2 weeks, a year, and so on. (Engineer)
Lack of university initiative. I had contact with some Engineering teachers recently. It was disappointing. Teachers were out of touch with reality. In our case of electrical engineering, you have to be attuned to the news. (Engineer)
The lack of opportunity. The university student has no opportunity to experiment, to venture. But it's not so tragic. If you chase, if you struggle, if you are persistent, if you are stubborn, you will go over the barrier. (Engineer)
The lack of time. Teachers seem to think that students only have that class they are ministering. They get excited and give a thousand things for the student to do. And this happens in all classes the students are taking. And so, instead of helping, they harm us, because students do not have time to think of anything different, do not have time to create. (Engineer)
There's no motivation. The teacher does not say: "Students, isn't there a better idea?" The teaching is one way. It is only from the teacher to students. He might even be offended if you express an opinion. (Engineering student)

Designing Stages of the
Teaching Practices Inventory

Aiming at capturing the largest number of elements to be taken into account in the preparation of the instrument items, a review of research on creativity in educational contexts was conducted, focusing especially on studies of creativity in the university classroom. Nineteen items developed by Alencar (1995c) to assess the degree of the incentives for the development and expression of creative abilities of students by university professors were included. These items were used in several studies with both samples of undergraduate and graduate students (Alencar, 1995c, 1997b, 2002c). This instrument was designed to be answered by students considering university professors in general, rather than a specific professor. This generated criticism from respondents who highlighted differences between their professors with regard to behaviors related to issues that were being investigated.

Other items were subsequently developed based on results from one particular study, conducted by Alencar (2000b), about the university professor facilitator and inhibitor of creativity, in which two open questions were used to raise the profile of these professors according to graduate students. At first, the student was asked to select from among his or her professors the one who offered the best conditions for the development and expression of creative abilities of their students. Next, the student would submit a more detailed description of the possible behaviors typical of this professor in the classroom, the way he treats the students both in and out of class, the teaching methods used by the teacher selected, his degree of preparation and interest in the matter under his responsibility in the program, and other data that could be considered relevant about the professor. In the next question, the same data was asked, but in relation to the inhibitor professor. It was noted that the aspects most discussed in the description of the professor were instructional techniques, professor preparedness, quality of professor-student relationship, interest in the subject and the student's learning, and personality traits.

So, the Teaching Practices Inventory was developed with 37 items, elaborated in three versions: two to be answered by the professor—one considering his or her typical behaviors in the classroom and the other the response of his or her students in evaluating teaching behaviors in the classroom—and a third version to be completed by the student evaluating his or her professor. It should be noted that the items of the three versions of the scale are the same. The only difference is in the instructions provided to the respondent, as shown in Figure 1.

Each item is answered on a 5-point scale, ranging from "strongly disagree" to "strongly agree." Accompanying the instrument on the first page, with instructions on how to answer it, is the survey respondent's biographical data. The final page contains a space for comments and observations that the respondent considers pertinent.

A pilot study was conducted to semantically analyze the items in order to ensure their understanding and avoid ambiguity and less appropriate formulations. To this end, the instrument was administered to eight classes (seven in public universities and one in a private university), asking respondents to indicate if there were confusing or ambiguous items. One hundred and thirty two students and seven teachers responded to the instrument.

Immediately after this step, procedures were put in place to reformulate two items and add another. These procedures resulted in 38 items that made up the instrument before establishing its construct validity.

Validation of the Teaching Practices Inventory

The instrument was administered to a sample of 1,068 college students for statistical validation. Six hundred and twelve were female (57.3%) and 449 students (42%) were male. Seven students (0.7%) did not answer this question. Of the 1,068 students, 599 (56.1%) were studying courses in the sciences while 467 (43.7%) were students in humanities. Two students (0.2%) did not indicate which courses they took. Six hundred and eight (56.9%) students were enrolled in private institutions of higher education and 459 students (43%) attended a public institution. One student did not answer the question (0.1%). The majority of students (n=731) participating in the study attended the first half of the course (68.4%) and 323 (30.2%) students were in the second half of the course. Among students, 14 (1.3%) did not report how many semesters they had attended. The average age of the students was 23.97, ranging from 16 to 68 years old.

Coordinators and/or professors of different courses were contacted in order to request their assistance in the project. Also, research assistants

Teacher—"As a professor of _____, is my typical behavior in the classroom (. . .)" and "According to the students of _____, is my typical behavior in the classroom (. . .)".

Student—"In _____, the professor generally (. . .)"

FIGURE 1. *Differences in instructions provided to respondents.*

collaborated by identifying and contacting university professors who would be available to participate. The administration of the instrument was performed by undergraduate students trained for this task. Confidentiality of responses was assured to the participants.

Of the instruments administered, 807 were used for validation purposes, because the other respondents did not get to complete them. To establish the construct validity of the instrument, its internal structure was verified through factor analysis. Using the SPSS statistical package, an analysis of the axis was done (Principle Axis Factoring), with oblique rotation, after having checked the normality of distributions and the assumptions of factor analysis.

Five factors were extracted based on the Kaiser criterion (Gable & Wolf, 1993), in that the *eigenvalue* of the factor should be equal to or more than 1. The five-factor solution explained 49.9% of common variance. However, one factor was dropped because it included only one item. This item (Item 15: Give students time to think and develop new ideas) was not allocated on any of the remaining factors and was, therefore, eliminated. In addition, we integrated only items with factor loading equal to or greater than 0.30. The four factors identified by the analysis are described below. Therefore, the final version of the instrument included 37 items.

Factor 1–Incentive to New Ideas

Factor 1, named Incentive to New Ideas, includes 14 items related to the fostering of cognitive abilities and affective characteristics associated with student's creativity. The *eigenvalue* of this factor was 15.72, explaining 40.14% of the common variance. The alpha internal-consistency coefficient was .93. The items of this factor, together with their factor loadings, are presented in Table 11.

Factor 2–Climate for Expression of Ideas

This factor includes six items that relate specially to the teacher's attitude of respect and acceptance about the ideas presented by students (see Table 12). The *eigenvalue* of this factor was 1.89, explaining 3.75% of the common variance. The alpha internal-consistency coefficient was .72.

Factor 3–Evaluation and Teaching Methodology

Factor 3, named Evaluation and Teaching Methodology, encompasses five items regarding teaching practices conducive to the development of creative expression (see Table 13). The *eigenvalue* of this factor was 1.54, explaining 2.56% of the common variance. The alpha internal-consistency coefficient was .85.

Factor 4–Interest for Students' Learning

Factor 4, named Interest for Students' Learning, includes 12 items regarding teaching strategies and resources that motivate students to learn in a creative way (see Table 14). The *eigenvalue* of this factor was 1.26, explaining 2.06% of the common variance. The alpha internal-consistency coefficient was .72.

Research Carried Out With the Inventory of Pedagogical Practices for Creativity in Higher Education

The Teaching Practices Inventory has been used in studies on creativity, such as the ones conducted by Alencar and Fleith (2004b), Ribeiro and Fleith (2007), and Sathler (2007). Alencar and Fleith (2004b) asked college students from public and private institutions to evaluate the extent to which their professors presented behaviors in the classroom that fostered students' creative development and expression. Professors were also requested to assess their own teaching practices in relation to creativity. The results indicated a discrepancy between professors' and students' perceptions on the extent to which teachers displayed favorable behaviors to

TABLE 11

Factor Loadings of the Items Comprising Factor 1
(Incentive to New Ideas)

Item	Content	Factor Loading
3	Encourages students to examine different aspects of a problem.	.85
10	Guides students to know and understand different points of view on the same issue or topic of study.	.78
2	Asks challenging questions that motivate students to think and to reason.	.72
9	Develops students' critical analysis skills.	.71
5	Encourages students to think of new ideas regarding the content of the discipline.	.66
4	Encourages students' initiative.	.62
7	Stimulates students' curiosity through the proposed tasks.	.56
1	Cultivates in students interest concerning new discoveries and new knowledge.	.54
12	Encourages students to ask questions concerning the topics studied.	.53
8	Encourages students' independence.	.52
6	Promotes students' self-confidence.	.48
17	Presents various aspects of an issue that is being studied.	.45
20	Asks questions, seeking connections to the topics studied.	.36
19	Promotes debates to encourage the participation of all students.	.33

Note. Eigenvalue = 15.72. Number of items = 14.

promote the development of creativity in the classroom. The professors' evaluation was much more positive than the students' evaluation. It was also observed that Evaluation and Teaching Methodology was the factor with the lowest average. Female students evaluated their professors more favorably in the factors Incentive to New Ideas and Interest for Students'

TABLE 12

Factor Loadings of the Items Comprising Factor 2
(Climate for Expression of Ideas)

Item	Content	Factor Loading
14	Creates an environment of respect and acceptance of students' ideas.	.61
33	Listens carefully to students' interventions.	.60
15	Provides students a chance to disagree with the teacher's points of view.	.57
34	Is not attentive to the students' interests.	.55
36	Has a sense of humor in the classroom.	.41
11	Values students' original ideas.	.39

Note. Eigenvalue = 1.89. Number of items = 6.

TABLE 13

Factor Loadings of the Items Comprising Factor 3
(Evaluation and Teaching Methodology)

Item	Content	Factor Loading
16	Uses evaluation strategies that require only the reproduction of content given in class or in the adopted books.	.70
18	Always uses the same teaching method.	.64
29	Provides students little choice about the assignments to be developed.	.50
13	Is solely concerned with the information content.	.47
26	Makes use of diversified strategies of evaluation.	.37

Note. Eigenvalue = 1.54. Number of items = 5.

Learning, comparing to male students. Furthermore, students who were in the second half of the course rated their professors more positively in regard to Incentive to New Ideas and Evaluation and Teaching Methodology compared to students who were in the first half of the course.

Ribeiro and Fleith (2007) also investigated the extent to which 82 professors of teaching education courses considered that their practices favored

TABLE 14

Factor Loadings of the Items Comprising Factor 4
(Interest for Students' Learning)

Item	Content	Factor Loading
31	Offers important and interesting information regarding the academic discipline content.	.58
28	Exposes the contents in a didactic manner.	.57
37	Presents updated content.	.53
30	Gives constructive feedback to students.	.51
21	Uses examples to illustrate the content taught in class.	.50
22	Is ready to clear students' doubts.	.48
32	Has enthusiasm toward the content taught.	.46
35	Has positive expectations regarding students' performance.	.44
24	Arouses the students' interest through the content being taught.	.41
27	Presents problem situations to be resolved by students.	.39
25	Is available to meet students outside the classroom.	.36
23	Provides extensive bibliography on the topics covered.	.35

Note. Eigenvalue = 1.26. Number of items = 12.

the development of their students' creativity. The study also included the participation of 1,396 students. The results indicated that the professors' perceptions of their teaching practices were more favorable than the students' perceptions. Furthermore, advanced semester students evaluated their professors' practices in relation to creativity more positively compared to the students from the first semesters. Differences among private and public university students' perceptions of their professors' practices were also observed in the factors Incentive to New Ideas and Evaluation and Teaching Methodology, with the private university students' perceptions more favorable.

In a recent study conducted by Sathler (2007), the Teaching Practices Inventory was adapted for use in the context of distance education. The factors generated were: Development of Creative Learning, Climate for the Development and Expression of Ideas, Incentive to Creative Thinking and Personality, and Content Assessment. The purpose of the study was to investigate 122 university students' perceptions of practices that foster creativity in a distance learning course through the use of the adapted inventory. The results revealed that, according to the students, their tutors implemented pedagogical practices that fostered the development of their creative abilities. The pedagogical practices more positively evaluated were those related to climate for the development and expression of ideas.

Final Considerations

The Teaching Practices Inventory constitutes a useful instrument for research and diagnostic of teaching behaviors that promote the development and expression of higher education students' creative abilities. Its factors refer to several professors' attributes, to the dynamics of their teaching practice, and to professors' interest in students and their learning. These are features included in the strategies suggested by different creativity experts, such as Torrance (1970, 1987, 1995), Cropley (1997; Cropley & Urban, 2000), Renzulli (1992), Fleith (2001), and Alencar (2001a, 2002a), to promote creativity in the classroom. A satisfactory degree of internal consistency and an expressive item-total correlation were observed in several factors of the instrument.

Besides its application to research, the instrument can also be used to give professors feedback on their teaching practices as perceived by students. The instrument can also be administered to complement data collected through a teacher's observation in the classroom and/or interview, helping to eliminate bias (Gall, Borg, & Gall, 1996).

It is noteworthy that the focus of this chapter was on the teaching practices of university professors. The teacher, no doubt, plays an important role in the process of helping students to develop their potential and to acquire desirable skills for their personal and professional achievement, as pointed out by numerous authors, like Alencar (2001a), Cropley (1997), Furman (1998), Sternberg (1991), and Tan (2001), among others. However, it is important to remember that there are other factors that contribute to what happens in the classroom, with impact on teachers' behaviors and practices. The nature of the content being taught, the number of students in class, and the degree of students' motivation and effort are elements that influence classroom dynamics. Knowledge about the impact of different variables on the development and expression of creativity in the educational context is still limited.

Creativity is a complex and pluridetermined phenomenon. Numerous individual and environmental characteristics contribute to enhance or inhibit creativity development and expression. Elements of the several environments where the individual is inserted, such as family and school, besides societal factors, impact the expression of creativity. Moreover, as pointed out by Sternberg and Lubart (1995), the type of environment that facilitates the development and realization of the creative potential depends on many factors, such as, for example, the individual's interests, his or her level of creative potential, knowledge background, and availability of time to devote to a specific area. Furthermore, the interaction among the multiple factors that influence the expression of creativity is highly complex.

It's hoped that the instrument presented in this chapter contributes to the advancement of knowledge and practices on creativity, especially in the educational context. As quoted by Castanho (2000, p. 76), "schools need to change. Present times require a broad and creative culture, which permeates all action in society, spreading to all institutions." Smith-Bingham (2006) extended this idea by stating that "universities should be regarded as repositories of knowledge and research that have enormous potential to innovate" (p. 17). Therefore, it is important to have an educational agenda that prioritizes the development of creative abilities and makes teachers aware of their role in this process.

CHAPTER 5

ASSESSMENT OF CREATIVITY IN MATHEMATICS

Cleyton Hércules Gontijo and Denise de Souza Fleith

I n many countries, educational policies have guided the formulation of school curricula that can stimulate the creative potential of students. This usually occurs once the development of creative abilities is considered an element that encourages people to present innovative solutions for the problems that actually emerge as a result of new social, economic, and technological challenges.

Among the distinct areas of knowledge that have a strict relationship with the process of scientific and technological development, mathematics plays an important role because, besides contributing especially in computing and engineering, it is not restricted to these areas, with increasing inroads in the humanities, social, and biological sciences constituting a path for the construction of measurement instruments, validation of observations, and preparation of models for the explanation of the social fact. According to the National Curriculum Parameters for Secondary Education (PCNEM; Brazil, 1999),

> It is possible that there is no contemporary life activity, from music to computing, from business to meteorology, from medicine to cartography, from engineering to communications, in which Mathematics are not present in an irreplaceable way to encode, sort, quantify and interpret bar, rates, measurements, coordinates, voltages, frequencies and so many other existing variables. (pp. 21–22)

Given the importance of this area of knowledge, mathematics is present in the curricula of education systems in Brazil in elementary and secondary school. This presence is justified in terms of contributions that mathematics can provide to a citizen's education, because "the understanding and decision making in the face of political and social issues depend on critical reading and interpreting complex information, often contradictory, which include statistical data and indices published by the media" (Brazil, 1998, p. 27).

That is, diverse skills are necessary for the full exercise of citizenship, including how to calculate, measure, reason, argue, and deal with statistical information, which can be developed from situations related to the field of mathematics. However, despite its importance in various areas of knowledge as well as in daily life, the learning processes of the discipline have been characterized as complex. For example, among the barriers that Brazil has faced in relation to mathematics teaching are the deficiencies in teacher training, the restrictions referring to the working conditions of teachers, the lack of educational projects, and the misinterpretations of pedagogical conceptions. These barriers explain the unsatisfactory performance of students, revealed by the high rates of failure in mathematics, which can actually act as a social filter at the elementary school level, selecting those who may or may not be able to conclude this level of education.

To include the development of creativity as one of the purposes of pedagogical work in mathematics can, according to Tobias (2004), collaborate to overcome the anxiety involved in mathematics learning, besides breaking barriers that inhibit success in this area. Moreover, according to the author, it offers teacher and students a new dynamic in the space/time of mathematics learning, providing to both the mathematical experience of creation, modeling, and explaining the object of study. He added that the development of creativity in mathematics allows rethinking this area as a professional career because, nowadays, it has attracted few young people.

Within our home country, the National Curriculum Parameters for mathematics propose creativity as one of the elements associated with the goals of this subject at various stages of basic education (Brazil, 1997, 1998, 1999). However, in the Parameters there is not a basic definition of what creativity or creative potential is in order to establish strategies for its development. No guidance on how to recognize and evaluate students' creative production is presented.

From the observation that there are no official documents in Brazil regarding how to stimulate creativity in the field of mathematics, we developed this study with the purpose of presenting a concept of creativity in mathematics and an instrument to assess this kind of creativity. We hope to contribute to the improvement of curriculum guidelines in this area, subsidizing Brazilian educators and those in other countries in organizing activities that will foster students' creativity as well as giving them tools to identify talent in mathematics.

Creativity in Mathematics

We have found that Brazilian literature has already a significant number of studies that deal with creativity and factors that can promote or inhibit its development. However, with respect to creativity in specific areas of school curriculum, the literature is incipient, especially in relation to mathematics.

On the other hand, in the international literature there are many references concerning the development and assessment of creativity in mathematics (Hashimoto, 1997; Haylock, 1985, 1987, 1997; Livne, Livne, & Milgram, 1999; Livne & Milgram, 2000; Muir, 1988; Sheffield, 2003; Silver, 1985, 1994, 1997; Silver & Cai, 1996; Sriraman, 2004). These studies, beyond describing the creative process in mathematics, have privileged the problem definition and resolution and the redefinition of mathematical entities as didactic-methodological strategies that allow the development and analysis of creativity in this area. Among the papers produced in Brazil in respect to creativity in mathematics, we suggest the ones by

Dante (1980, 1988) related to creativity and problem resolution, and the D'Ambrosio (2004) paper in which the author presented a model explaining creativity in mathematics.

One of the research challenges in creativity in mathematics is finding a consensus for what characterizes this type of ability. In order to understand it, several authors attempted to differentiate some types of mathematical ability, classifying them as "academic" ability and "creative" ability (Krutetskii, 1976; Livne & Milgram, 2006; Poincaré, 1908/1996, 1911/1995).

Livne and Milgram (2006), for example, referred to academic abilities as a type of general intelligence applied to mathematics that reflects logical thinking, demonstrated by calculation abilities, domain concepts, mathematics principles and fundamentals, and the capacity to present plausible arguments through mathematical reasoning. This type of ability is required in situations that have a unique way to solve the problem. For the authors, creative ability is characterized by the patterns and relationships using complex thinking (not algorithmic thinking) and by the capacity of presenting original thinking utilizing mathematical symbols that results in many strategic resolutions or correct answers.

Interested in creative abilities in the field of mathematics and considering the literature in the area, Gontijo (2006) defined creativity in mathematics as "the capacity of presenting several solutions that are appropriate for a problem so that these focus on different aspects of the problem and/or different forms of solving it" (p. 4). This ability can be employed both in situations that require a resolution and an elaboration of the problem, like in situations that demand a classification or organization of objects and/or mathematical elements according to their properties and attributes, in textual, numerical, or graphic format or in a sequence of actions.

Creative production in mathematics could also be characterized by the abundance or quantity of different ideas produced about a topic (fluency), by the capacity of altering the thinking and conceiving different categories of answers (flexibility), by presenting infrequent or unusual answers (originality), and by presenting great quantities of details in an idea (elaboration). Thus, for the stimulation and development of creativity, a climate that allows the student to present fluency, flexibility, originality, and elaboration must be cultivated (Alencar, 2000c).

Beyond these characteristics, other variables are presented in the creative process, such as many mental operations (e.g., abstract thinking, inductive and deductive reasoning, analogical, metaphoric, and intuitive thinking). Emotional elements are also important for this process (Alencar, 2000c).

It is emphasized that creative production, in any area of knowledge, must be understood and nurtured from a vision that transcends the characteristics of each person, because "one cannot simply consider the operations of the creative person's mind. One must also explore the interaction between the mind and the symbolic system of the domain, and the social constraints and opportunities of the field" (Nakamura & Csikszentmihalyi, 2003, p. 187). Thus, one must consider creativity as the result of a process in which three systems interact dialectically (Csikszentmihalyi, 1988, 1999): the individual (genetic background and personal experience), domain of knowledge (cultural and scientific production), and field (social system that evaluates the ideas produced).

Assessment of Creativity in Mathematics

Balka (1974) established some criteria to measure creativity in mathematics, indicating abilities to be assessed. These abilities are:
- ability to formulate mathematical hypotheses evaluating cause and effect relationships in mathematical situations;
- ability to consider and evaluate unusual mathematical ideas, reflecting on their impact on mathematical situations;
- ability to perceive problems from a mathematical situation and formulate questions that can answer these problems;
- ability to define specific subproblems from a general mathematical problem;
- ability to seek solutions to mathematical problems, breaking from a "static" mental picture; and
- ability to develop models to solve mathematical situations.

The indication of these abilities inspired the development of many tests for assessing mathematical creativity. But most of the published tests do not provide data regarding their validity and reliability. However, these tests serve to illustrate types of situations or problems that may be developed with students in order to develop creative thinking. Foster (1970) developed two tests to assess the creative abilities in mathematics for students between the ages of 9 and 11 years old. In the first test, the child selects six cards from a deck that have something in common. Points are counted according to the number of sets made in 5 minutes. The second test asks the child to find how many total sets are possible using the numbers 2, 3, and 6 and the four operations.

Another test to measure mathematical creativity and to identify mathematical talent in students between the ages of 11 and 13 was proposed by Singh (1987). One of the activities of the test asks the student to write integers from 1 to 5 using four "sevens" and associating them to the various operations known. The number 10, for example, can be written as (77-7)/7. This activity requires the student to discover the different expressions that correspond to the numbers given. In another activity (see Figure 2), students are given different and unique values to letters of the alphabet, so that the results of the operation indicated are correct.

This activity allows students to establish new relationships, because when given arbitrary and different values for B and D, they determine the values of R, and when given different values for A and C, nonequivalent to B, D, and R, they determine the values of K and P, because these are not the same data as B, D, R, A, and C.

Likewise, Mednick, quoted by Dunn (1975), created an item that asks students to write as many real equations as possible with three numbers given in order and an equal sign. For this, we can use, if necessary, the symbols +, -, x, ÷, (). The author illustrated the solution of the problem, indicating that the students should use the numbers 2, 3, and 8. Some possible answers are shown in Figure 3.

This item has a similar structure to one of the items of the test that was proposed by Singh (1987), mentioned earlier.

Another tool for assessing mathematical creativity was developed by Haylock (1987), who produced several tests to investigate mathematical creativity in 11- and 12-year-old students. In one test, the instruction given was to "write down what the numbers 16 and 36 have in common." According to Haylock, an 11-year-old student made several statements about the numbers, such as:

they are divisible by two, they are divisible by four, they are smaller than 40, they contain 6 as the last digit, they are greater than 15,

A B

            + C D

—————————

PKR

FIGURE 2. *Activity that measures mathematical creativity.*

$2^3 - 8 = 0$
$2 \times 3 + 8 = 14$
$2 \div 3 \div 8 = 1/12$

FIGURE 3. *Possible answers to Mednick's item.*

they are integers, they are factors of 576, they are not primes, they are square numbers, they are in this question. (p. 59)[*]

In another test, students were asked to find as many pictures as possible to build, within a 2 cm² area, connecting the dots in a square grid formed by nine points, with the distance between two consecutive points in the horizontal or vertical equal to 1 cm. The flexibility, fluency, and originality of the student responses were used as indicators of creative abilities in mathematics.

Also Lee, Hwang, and Seo (2003) developed an instrument to assess the ability of Korean high school students to solve mathematical problems in a creative way. The authors proposed five items, assessing fluency, flexibility, and originality of the responses provided by 462 students from gifted and regular high schools in Korea. The alpha coefficient reliability of the instrument was .80. Furthermore, they indicated an index of difficulty and discriminating power of the items.

In addition to tests that assess creativity in mathematics, there was a validation study of a scale measuring the activities and interests in mathematics, developed by Livne and Milgram (2000), which investigated the

---

[*]   Haylock, D.W. (1987). A framework for assessing mathematical creativity in school children. *Educational Studies in Mathematics, 18*, 59–74. [With kind permission from Springer Science+Business Media: *Educational Studies in Mathematics*, A framework for assessing mathematical creativity in school children, v. 18, 1987, p. 59, Dereck W. Haylock.]

level of involvement of Israeli students with mathematical activities that they performed outside of school. This study was conducted with a group of judges (experts, university professors, graduate students, and high school students who attended a school for highly talented students—all with a background in mathematics) and a group of students in 11th and 12th grades in public schools in urban areas of Israel. The research indicated that an instrument with 12 items, resulting from the confrontation between the responses of judges and students, could be used to measure activities and interests of students toward mathematics, indicating the extent to which these activities are related to creativity. According to the statement of the authors, the instrument contains all of the necessary elements to be considered capable of a reliable and valid representation for the four levels of creativity evaluated, namely the ordinary, mild, moderate, and profound.

The ordinary level would include those who have jobs who do not produce changes in the field of mathematics, because they use routine procedures that express low divergent thinking. These individuals demonstrate that their motivation comes from external sources, reflecting a mild commitment to their tasks and initiative. The degree of intensity with which they perform their tasks in mathematics is also low.

The mild level also includes people who produce little change in mathematics. They use more convergent than divergent thinking. They are more externally than internally motivated, reflecting a mild level commitment with respect to the tasks, initiative, and degree of intensity in carrying out their activities.

Those at a moderate level present the most challenging attitudes toward mathematics. They use more divergent thinking than convergent thinking and their activities generate products of unusual quality. They are more internally than externally motivated, reflecting moderate commitment to tasks and initiative, and the degree of intensity with which they implement their activities is also moderate.

The profound level contains those with highly challenging attitudes toward mathematics. They mainly use divergent thinking and their activities result in products of unusually high quality. They are internally motivated, reflecting high commitment to tasks, and have a great initiative. The degree of intensity with which they implement their activities is very high.

Creativity Test in Mathematics: A Proposal

The Creativity Test in Mathematics was developed for a study that aimed to examine the relationship between creativity, creativity in mathematics, and motivation in mathematics for high school students (Gontijo, 2007). It assesses three types of activities that enable the expression of creativity in mathematics: problem solving, problem formulation, and redefinition of elements (Haylock, 1987). The test has six items selected from published studies that presented some items to assess mathematical creativity (Haylock, 1985, 1987; Lee et al., 2003; Livne, Livne, & Milgram, 1999; Silver & Cai, 1996; Vasconcelos, 2002). The choice of these items came from successive administrations of an instrument, containing 15 items, in groups of high school and undergraduate students, noting: (a) the complexity of the situations presented to students, preventing them to require specific knowledge about a particular content; (b) the "acquaintance"of students with the types of activities proposed, since situation-problems that allow many solutions are not common in daily classes of mathematics; and (c) the necessary time for the production of a significant number of answers for each item, avoiding the selection of items that demanded a lot of time for a solution. A definition of objective criteria for evaluating fluency, flexibility, and originality categories was also observed through the choice of items.

The items that composed the test are:
- Some points are given below, so that the distance between them, both horizontally and vertically, is equal to 1 centimeter. Connecting these points, construct polygons that have perimeter (sum of the size of the sides) equal to 14 cm. Draw each polygon separately from the others (Vasconcelos, 2002).
- "Try to make the number 4, using precisely four times (not two times) the digit 4, which is an integer multiplication of the digit 2. Try to make the largest possible number of solutions that overall include all of the following arithmetic operations: addition, subtraction, multiplication, division, square root, factorial, and so on. In every solution separately, one need not use all the operations" (Livne & Milgram, 2006, p. 202).**

** Livne, N. L., & Milgram, R. M. (2006). Academic versus creative abilities in mathematics: Two components of the same construct? *Creativity Research Journal, 18,* 199–212. Reprinted by permission of the publisher (Taylor & Francis Lrd, http://www.tandf.co.uk/journals).

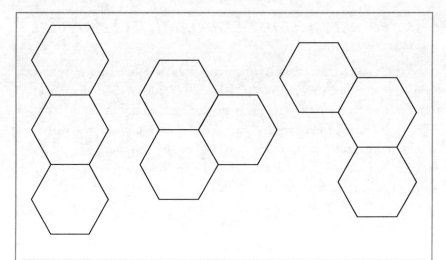

FIGURE 4. *Regular hexagons. Adapted from "A development of the test for mathematical creative problem solving ability," by K. S. Lee, D. Hwang, and J. J. Seo, 2003,* Journal of the Korea Society of Mathematical Education, 7, *p. 181. Reprinted with permission.*

- Develop different issues that can be answered from the following information: "Jerome, Elliot, and Arturo took turns driving home from a trip. Arturo drove 80 miles more than Elliot. Elliot drove twice as many miles as Jerome. Jerome drove 50 miles" (Silver & Cai, 1996, p. 525).***
- The illustrations in Figures 4 show examples using three regular hexagons formed by the union of its sides. Drawing upon the models in Figure 4, make as many figures as possible, using six figures in the form of a regular hexagon.
- Consider the integers from 2 to 16 (including 2 and 16) and write the number of subsets that you can establish involving those numbers, indicating the rule for the formation of each (i.e., indicating the characteristics that the numbers possess and that can be made in the same subset; Haylock, 1985, 1987).
- Consider the geometric solids shown in Figure 5. Choose one or more solids that share similar characteristics with figure B and write down these characteristics.

*** Reprinted by permission of the authors.

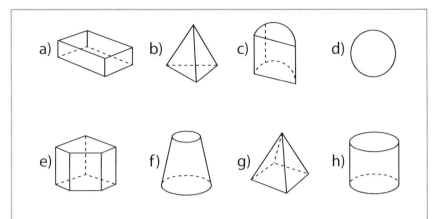

FIGURE 5. *Geometric solids. Adapted from "A development of the test for mathematical creative problem solving ability," by K. S. Lee, D. Hwang, and J. J. Seo, 2003,* Journal of the Korea Society of Mathematical Education, *7, p. 183. Reprinted with permission.*

The time limit to answer this instrument was 50 minutes, divided as follows: 5 minutes for the first item, 10 minutes for the second item, 10 minutes for the third item, 10 minutes for item 4, 5 minutes for item 5, and 10 minutes for item 6.

Criteria of Judging the Creativity Test in Mathematics Answers

Item 1

For the evaluation of answers referring to item 1, we adopted the following criteria:

- Fluency: the number of polygons drawn up to satisfy the conditions of the problem (to have a perimeter equal to 14 cm), which are not congruent (when superimposed, even necessary, for example, performing a rotation in one of them that is not identical).
- Flexibility: number of categories of polygons, designed according to the area of polygons.
- Originality: the relative rarity of polygons.

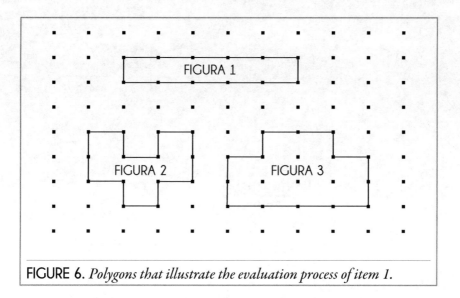

FIGURE 6. *Polygons that illustrate the evaluation process of item 1.*

The following example illustrates the process of evaluating responses for this item; for this, consider the polygons in Figure 6.

The first figure has an area equal to 6 cm^2; the second, an area equal to 6 cm^2; and the third, an area of 10 cm^2. Thus:

- fluency has a value of 3 because it has built three different polygons with perimeter equal to 14 cm;
- flexibility has a value of 2, built for polygons with area 6 cm^2 and 10 cm^2, and
- originality's value depends on the analysis of the results of all study participants and will be scored if the student has built at least one polygon that no one else has built.

According to Smith (1990), a total of 137 different polygons can be obtained with a perimeter equal to 14 cm, so that four of these polygons have an area equal to 4 cm^2, 12 polygons have an area equal of 5 cm^2, 38 have an area equal to 6 cm^2, 32 have an area equal to 7 cm^2, 30 have an area equal to 8 cm^2, 12 have an area equal to 9 cm^2, 7 have an area equal to 10 cm^2, one has an area of 11 cm^2, and one polygon measures 12 cm^2.

Item 2

For the evaluation of item 2 answers, the following criteria were used:

- Fluency: the number of mathematical sentences involving four iterations of the number 4 only, and with a result equal to 4.
- Flexibility: the number of categories of sentences, calculated by the number of different operations used in each sentence.
- Originality: the relative rarity of the sentences.

The following example illustrates the process of evaluating the answers to item 2:

(a) $\sqrt{4} + 4 + 4 + 4 = 4$
(b) $(4-4) \times 4 + 4 = 4$
(c) $\sqrt{4} + \sqrt{4} - 4 + 4 = 4$
(d) $4! - (4 \times 4) - 4 = 4$
(e) $4\sqrt{4} - \sqrt{4} - \sqrt{4} = 4$
(f) $4! \div 4 + \sqrt{4} - 4 = 4$
(g) $(4 \div 4) \times \sqrt{4} + \sqrt{4} = 4$
(h) $(4! - 4 - 4) \div 4 = 4$

Thus:

- Fluency: Value = 8, because eight mathematical sentences involving only four numbers and producing results equal to 4 were produced.
- Flexibility: Considering the number of different operations performed on each answer, flexibility has a value of 3. The answers given for the letters were (a) to have used two different operations (addition and roots); in responses to letters (b), (c), (d), (e), and (h), three different types of operations in each one were used; in responses to the letters (f) and (g), four different types of operations were used in each one.
- Originality: This value depends on the analysis of the results of all study participants and will be scored if the student has built at least one sentence that no one has generated.

Item 3

For the evaluation of answers submitted to item 3, there were recommendations by Silver and Cai (1996), who described three steps for the judgement of the answers. The first step consists of classifying the responses into three categories: math question, not a math question, or a statement. Only the responses classified as math question should be considered for the purpose of evaluation. The second step consists of categorizing the mathematics questions into those that are solvable and nonsolvable. If the proposed problem omits required information or has questions inconsistent with the information given, this issue will be considered nonsolvable. The third step involves examining the complexity of the formulated problem.

One type of complexity refers to the syntactical structure involved in the problem. Such a structure is examined by focusing on the presence of a designative, relational, or conditional proposition. One example presented by the authors for a designed proposition is "All together, how many miles did they drive?" For the relational proposition, the following example is presented: "How many more miles did Arturo drive than Jerome?" and to exemplify a conditional proposition, there is the following question: "If Arturo went 80 kilometers more than Elliot, how many kilometers did Arturo drive?" (Silver & Cai, 1996, p. 527).

As for the semantic structure, the responses are analyzed considering five categories: change, group, comparison, variety, and replay.

The following criteria were defined for the evaluation of responses to item 3:

- Fluency: number of solvable math problems elaborated by students.
- Flexibility: number of categories according to the number of semantic relations involved in each response.
- Originality: the relative rarity of the proposed problems.

The questions below illustrate possible formulations that students can do:

(a) Did Arturo drive 80 kilometers more than Elliot?
(b) How many kilometers did Elliot drive?
(c) How many more kilometers did Arturo drive than Jerome?
(d) How many kilometers did all three drive together?
(e) How many times did they have to fill the car with fuel if the car has fuel for 60 km only?
(f) Did Arturo drive longer than Jerome and Elliot drove on a regular basis?

The evaluation indicates the following points:

- Fluency: value = 6, since there were six mathematical problems elaborated.

- Flexibility: value = 5. Question (a) has no semantic relationship. Question (b) has a relationship (replay) and question (c) has two (comparison and resubmission). As for question (d), there are three possible relations (group, replay, and replay). Question (e) indicates the presence of four relations (variety, group, replay, and replay) and question (f) presents five relations (comparison, representation, group, representation, and variety).
- Originality: infrequent responses, which will be considered using the data found.

Item 4

The fourth item asks students to draw pictures using six regular hexagons that must be joined by at least one of their sides. Thus, the analysis pointed out the following criteria.

- Fluency: number of illustrations produced, excluding those representing the same illustration, whether they suffer partial or total rotation.
- Flexibility: the number of categories formed by the illustrations, established according to the manner by which the hexagons are coupled to each other. The categories are formed according to the number of hexagons arranged in a linear or circular form. Those that are linear may have two, three, four, five, or six hexagons. In these illustrations, there are those that have asymmetrical shapes, those with a point of symmetry, and those with predominate linear segments.
- Originality: infrequent responses, which will be considered from all of the illustrations presented.

Models of reference for the analysis of responses were considered (see Figure 7; Lee et al., 2003).

Item 5

The analysis of item 5 complies with the following criteria:

- Fluency: total number of subsets formed with numbers from 2 to 16 (including 2 and 16).
- Flexibility: number of categories formed according to the characteristics of elements of each subset (e.g., even numbers/odd

(a) Illustrations that contain a circular array:

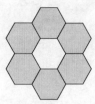

(b) Illustrations that contain two hexagons together on the same line

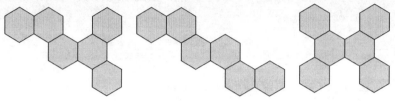

Asymmetrical   Symmetry Point   Line Segment

(c) Illustrations that contain three hexagons together in one line:

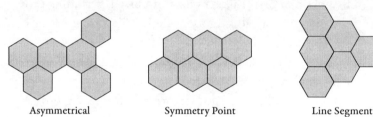

Asymmetrical   Symmetry Point   Line Segment

(d) Illustrations containing four hexagons together on the same:

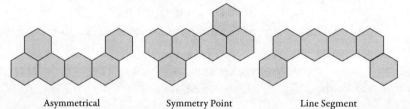

Asymmetrical   Symmetry Point   Line Segment

(e) Illustrations that contain five or more hexagons, together on the same line:

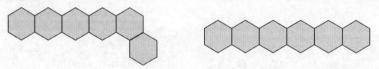

FIGURE 7. *Models of reference. Geometric solids. Adapted from "A development of the test for mathematical creative problem solving ability," by K. S. Lee, D. Hwang, and J. J. Seo, 2003,* Journal of the Korea Society of Mathematical Education, 7. *Reprinted with permission.*

	Subset	Rule	Error
A	1, 3, 5, 7, 9, 11, 13, 15	Odd numbers	1 included
B	2, 4, 6, 8, 10, 12, 14, 16	Even numbers	
C	3, 6, 9, 12, 15	Divisible by 3	
D	4, 8, 12, 16	Divisible by 4	
E	2, 3, 7, 11, 13	Prime numbers	5 not included
F	4, 5, 6, 8, 9, 10, 12, 14, 15, 16	Non-prime numbers	5 included
G	2, 3, 4, 5, 6, 7, 8, 9	Less than 10	
H	11, 12, 13, 14, 15, 16	More than 10	
I	2, 4, 8, 16	Divisors of 32	

Evaluation Criteria

Fluency: value = 6. Among the nine subsets produced, only six were correct according to the norms stated.

Flexibility: value = 5. Subsets A and B are complementary, thus, account for only one point. The same applies to the subsets G and H.

Originality: infrequent subsets, which will be considered from the all subsets presented.

FIGURE 8. *Subsets.*

numbers, multiply/divide, more than/less than, primes, negation or intersection of various attributes).

- Originality: relative rarity of produced subsets.

An example of evaluation of responses to this item is shown in Figure 8.

Item 6

Item 6 asks students to establish any relationship between the geometric figures (solid and plain) shown, whereas figure B should be part of all relationships created. Lee and collegues (2003) presented eight categories under which these solids would fall due to their characteristics: the shape of their faces (sides or bottom); numbers of edges, vertices, faces, angles, and relationships between them; a form of projection, shape from a section; a pyramid, formed from the development of a solid; volume; and others. These categories are the base for scoring flexibility, so that only one point for each category type will be counted. The fluency score is given based on the number of correct answers given by students. Originality is analyzed in terms of responses that were not frequently observed in all of the administered instruments.

Assessment of Creativity in Mathematics for High School Students

The Creativity Test in Mathematics was used in an investigation conducted by Gontijo (2007), especially considering three aspects: (a) whether there are differences between male and female students with respect to creativity in mathematics, (b) if there is a relationship between creativity, as measured by the Torrance Tests of Creative Thinking (TTCT; Torrance, 1974, 1990), and math, and (c) if there is a relationship between motivation in mathematics, as measured by the Motivation Scale in Mathematics (Gontijo, 2007), and creativity mathematics.

One hundred and ten high school juniors from a private school in Brasilia, Brazil, participated in this study. These students constituted the total enrollment of juniors in this school. However, the study included only students who answered all of the instruments that were administered, a total of 100 students.

The mean age of the participating students in the study was 17.06 years old, varying from 16 to 18 years of age. Fifty students were male and 50 were female. The school in which the study was held includes students from middle and upper socioeconomic status.

Some Results . . .

We present here some results found in this research. The full description can be seen in Gontijo (2007), which includes the statistical analysis and discussion of results in light of the literature. One of the important contributions of this study refers to the evidence that there is a positive correlation between creativity and creativity in mathematics. This data allows us to conclude that investments in creativity programs, training, and techniques in school can, to some extent, encourage the development of the creative potential of students in specific areas of the curriculum. An important finding of the study refers to the fact that students of both genders have similar creative potential, as evidenced by the results in the Torrance Tests of Creative Thinking. This result supports the idea that there is not superiority of men over women and vice versa on creativity measures. Opportunities and socialization processes are key elements for creativity development.

But if one part of this study found no significant differences between genders with regard to creativity, differences appeared with respect to creativity in mathematics in favor of male students. One of the difficulties in understanding these differences is due the lack of research focusing on gender issues regarding mathematical creativity. However, studies dealing with the assessment of academic skills in mathematics indicate that gender differences exist. One explanation for these differences may be associated with the type of stimulation received in childhood, driving boys to the outside world and girls to domestic activities (Kerr, 2000; Whitaker, 1995).

The results also indicated a positive correlation between mathematics motivation and creativity. This implies the need for building a culture of success, learning, and pleasure with respect to mathematics, so creative production in this field may occur with greater frequency and quality.

Final Considerations

To encourage creative productions in the school environment, mathematics teachers should use problem situations to organize the pedagogical work, offering challenging activities based both in the context as experienced by students and in abstract situations that require the use of a formal language and procedures that are characteristics of mathematics. Thus, activities involving problem design and solving, as well as the redefinition of mathematical elements, can become a valuable teaching resource for mathematics learning and for fostering creativity in this area.

The strategies aimed at fostering creativity should be chosen based on a consistent theoretical framework. In this sense, the Perspective of Systems by Csikszentmihalyi (1988, 1999) offers a unique contribution to understanding how the creative process occurs, indicating that this is a result of the dialectical interaction between three systems: person, field, and domain. In this regard, this study provides the possibility of applying this theory to the field of mathematics.

Regarding the assessment of mathematical creativity, it is necessary to develop instruments in order to implement comparative studies between different groups of students, examining which type of support offered to each group produces differences in students' creative productions. For this, case studies can be designed by controlling variables such as school type (public/private), study habits, students' income, age, gender, location, psychological school climate, teacher support, family support, etc. These instruments can also be used to analyze not only creativity as a product, but also as a process. The researcher may administer it individually, recording all of the actions of the respondent, as well as interacting with the student to understand the origin of his or her problem-solving strategies.

CHAPTER 6

INDICATORS OF THE CLIMATE FOR CREATIVITY IN THE WORKPLACE

Maria de Fátima Bruno-Faria

I n the previous chapters, the importance of creativity in the school environment was highlighted. In the organizational context, this scenario is not different. Creativity has great relevance, especially due to the current phenomenon of innovation. The recognition of the necessity of actions to produce innovation in different organizational contexts can be verified from the creation of laws establishing measures of incentives for innovation and scientific research by the Brazilian government (Financiadora de Estudos e Projetos [FINEP], 2004). A more productive and stimulating environment for innovations is desired in our home country.

Although the importance of creativity is recognized, especially because it generates innovations, a lot still needs to be done in many organizations regarding the adoption of strategies that encourage people to create in the workplace.

Scientific literature about this theme is still scarce in Brazil and has advanced very little in terms of theoretical production, as highlighted by Bruno-Faria, Veiga, and Macêdo (2008), in revising the publications in the period from 1996 to 2007. These scholars found only 17 articles published in Brazilian scientific journals, 12 papers in major scientific events in the area of management, and 11 books or chapters, only two of them having scientific basis, specifically discussing creativity in the organizational context. Research in the field of management predominates in the country, with few in the psychology of work.

Creativity is a complex phenomenon that requires a multidisciplinary approach. Such complexity demands diverse methodological strategies in order to understand its several facets. This includes factors related to the individuals and groups, the working environment, as well as the external environment that impact the organization's mode of action, as suggested by several scholars (Bruno-Faria, 2005; Lubart, 2007; Runco, 2007).

In this chapter, the focus is on the internal environment of the organization. It aims to describe a measure of the climate for creativity in the workplace, which intends to capture a set of elements of this reality that can interfere with the expression of the employees' creativity. It's believed that, from the application of this tool, a diagnosis can be made of the conditions of the work environment that favor the planning of actions that may facilitate professionals' creative expression in different work realities.

Creativity and Innovation: Differentiations and Interrelations Between Concepts

Creativity has been conceptualized in different ways, as highlighted by Alencar (1997a), who pointed out the existence of hundreds of definitions of the construct since 1950, when interest in the issue surged. This is a phenomenon dependent on the context. This means that to understand creativity in different realities, it is necessary to adopt different measures for its evaluation. When it refers to the world of work, creativity is often associated with the generation of something new or the improvement of something that may help the organization with the addition of some type of value. Typically, this value is associated with the results that the organization seeks to achieve with its strategies.

Regarding innovation, national and international scientific literature is more diverse and abundant. It seeks to address the specificities of its occurrence, in different taxonomies to represent types of innovations, such as innovation in product and process, administrative innovation, technical or technological innovations, etc. (Moreira & Queiroz, 2007).

Meanwhile, Fagerberg (2006) highlighted that innovation, while not a new phenomenon, has not received the attention it needs from academia. Yet, given its economic and social importance, it has been the focus of much more interest than creativity in the organizational context. This includes a variety of theories in the field of economy and administration.

Different authors have treated creativity as a necessary condition for the occurrence of innovation. Burnside, Amabile, and Gryskiewicz (1988), for example, emphasized that: "Creativity . . . is the production of new associations (new ideas) that are useful; innovation . . . is the successful implementation of useful new ideas" (p. 170).

Bruno-Faria (2003) took the same position on the importance of differentiating between the concepts of creativity and innovation in a comprehensive literature review of the concepts of creativity, innovation, and organizational change. The author presented definitions for each of these concepts, and proposed a model of interrelating them, in addition to discussing the specificities of each one.

The concept of creativity in organizations that Bruno-Faria (2003) came to, from her analysis, is presented below:

> Creativity is the generation of ideas, processes, products, and/or new services (for the individual, group or in a specific context) that produce some valuable contribution to the organization and/or the welfare of persons working in that context and that possess the essential elements for their implementation. (p. 117)

In this concept, creativity is seen as a process that may enable innovation, meaning that it is not enough to have just novelty and value in what it is produced, it is also necessary for it to be capable of implementation. Additionally, innovation, according to Bruno-Faria (2003), is closely related to creativity, although it may be from different sources. Based on a review of the literature, the author considered innovation as the implementation of ideas, processes, products, or services, derived from the creativity of individuals or groups in the organization. However, not all creative ideas generate innovation, because there may be barriers or difficulties in the implementation process of the idea and it may not be carried forward.

Furthermore, innovations may have different intensities, which may lead to organizational changes with different impacts. However, Bruno-Faria (2003) noted that both innovations and changes may be originating not only from people in the organization, but from the external context of the organization. Organizational change is regarded as "any change, planned or unplanned, occurring in the organization due to internal and/or external factors to it, that impacts results and/or the relations between people at work" (Bruno-Faria, 2003, p. 128).

Creativity, innovation, and organizational change are closely related, meaning that individuals' and groups' creativity in the workplace can lead to innovations that, in turn, cause differentiated changes. Scholars who are concerned with distinguishing these concepts, like Amabile (1996a), consider this task important in order to be aware of the different factors involved in these processes (creativity and innovation) as a way to enable actions that may contribute to their management.

Measures of Creativity in the Context of Work

The scale to be described in this chapter was the first identified in Brazilian literature to evaluate stimuli and barriers to creativity in the workplace (Bruno-Faria, 1996; Bruno-Faria & Alencar, 1996, 1998). Subsequently, Crespo (2004) constructed a scale with the same designation: indicators of the climate for creativity, with the goal of mapping the variables of an organizational climate that promotes creativity in the workplace. Crespo's questionnaire was composed of the following indicators: (a) motivation and commitment; (b) dynamism and energy; (c) time for ideas; (d) freedom to create; (e) playfulness and humor; (f) support for ideas; (g) discussions and debates; (h) absence of conflict; (i) trust and frankness; (j) taking risks; (k) supporting innovation (l); salaries and benefits and (m) tolerance of differences. This scale was not submitted to the statistical validation process, but only submitted to judges' analysis. An agreement was observed among all those who evaluated the items. It is noteworthy that this measure lacks statistical tests showing its psychometric validity, according to the requirements outlined by Pasquali (2001), in the construction process of instruments.

More recently, a new scale was developed in Brazil by Parolin, Bosquetti, Chang, Albuquerque, and Santos (2007), with the purpose of identifying the necessary conditions for the occurrence of the creative process in organizations. The authors, from a social interactionist perspective, built an instrument that, after statistical validation, comprised 24 items representing five different factors. The factor that explains most of the variance of the instrument (26.08%) includes 14 items covering, among other aspects, the physical environment, recognition by others, benefits, and investment of the organization in supporting creativity. The second factor, with three items explaining 8.8% of the total variance of the instrument, entitled "interpersonal relationships," represents positive aspects (teamwork, trust climate in teams) and a negative aspect (a lot of rivalry in teams), in relation to creativity. The third factor, with two items (creativity and supportive routines, and spontaneity and work environment), has been labeled "the task environment" and accounts for 7.5% of the total variance. The fourth factor, "pressure and control," corresponds to 6.1% of the total variance, and the two component items are: "open environments control the integration" and "control over goals and results." The last factor, responsible for 5.5% of the total variance, was named "creativity blocks," and includes two items: "excessive work" and "stress in the workplace."

Parolin et al. (2007) highlighted that their study was a pioneering initiative in the field of research on creativity in organizations in Brazil. This seems to signal the difficulty of accessing the existent literature on the topic in the country, due to the fact that three articles briefly presenting the construction process of the instrument to be described in this chapter were published in 1996 and 1998 (Bruno-Faria, 1996; Bruno-Faria & Alencar, 1996, 1998).

In relation to the production of creativity measures in the organizational context in other countries, the number of measures is also scarce. Mathisen and Einarsen (2004) conducted a review of instruments designed to access "the internal environment of the organization and social climate in relation to creativity and innovation" (p. 120). The authors noted that, although various publications deal with the discussion of organizational aspects related to creativity and innovation, their article was the first to analyze and compare different measures of creativity.

Mathisen and Einarsen (2004) also stressed that "the concepts of creativity and innovation are highly related" and "both of the concepts deal with the production and implementation of new and appropriate ideas—in this case, within the organizational context" (p. 120). Therefore, they decided to revise the instruments for measuring creativity and innovation. These authors noted that they found some instruments developed for academic purposes only, and others with academic and commercial purposes. In Table 15, some key characteristics of the five instruments identified by these researchers are summarized.

Regarding KEYS, Mathisen and Einarsen (2004) noted that this instrument is also relevant to assess innovation, as creativity is considered the seed of all innovation. This position differs from the one assumed in this chapter, as the fact that creativity is considered a precondition for innovation does not mean that the same measures apply to both phenomena, because the conditions to create differ from the conditions for innovation.

In 1996, Bruno-Faria had already identified the KEYS scale, by the time the previous version called Work Environment Inventory (WEI; Hill & Amabile, 1993) and the SSSI (Siegel & Kaemmerer, 1978). Besides the five instruments described by Mathisen and Einarsen (2004), Bruno-Faria (1996) also analyzed the scale called The Jones Inventory of Barriers (JIB), developed by Rickards and Jones (1991). This instrument aims to identify factors that inhibit the creative process, promote employee self-knowledge, and serve as a vehicle for developing the organization.

Indicators of Climate for Creativity: Construction and Validation Process

The purpose of the instrument was to identify stimulants and obstacles to creativity in the workplace. We intended to construct a measure that could be applied in organizations with different characteristics and that, besides contributing to fill the huge gap on the subject in Brazil, would be useful to managers in assessing the conditions for creativity in the workplace. The instrument should be answered by employees at different levels and functions in the organization, so as to obtain the perceptions of the work environment from various perspectives.

TABLE 15

Rating Scales of Creativity and Organizational Innovation

Name and author of the tool	Objective	Number of items and scale of responses	Factors or dimensions
Siegel Scale of Support for Innovation (SSSI; Siegel & Kaemmerer, 1978)	Assess organizational climate factors assumed to be present in innovative organizations.	The instrument consists of 61 items. Likert scale response format with six response alternatives, ranging from strongly agree to strongly disagree.	It comprises five dimensions: » leadership, » ownership, » norms for diversity, » continued development, and » consistency.
KEYS (Amabile et al., cited in Mathisen & Einarsen, 2004)	Assess the workplace for creativity.	The instrument consists of 78 items. Response scale of 4 points (never or almost never, sometimes, often, always or almost always).	It consists of 10 scales. The first six refer to the encouragement of creativity; two more are named "organizational impediments" and "workload pressure," and are hypothesized to relate negatively with creativity; and two more criterion scales assess the perception of creativity and productivity in organizations. The stimulant scales are: » organizational encouragement, » supervisory encouragement, » work group support, » sufficient resources, » challenging work, and » freedom. The obstacle scales are: » organizational impediments, and » workload pressure. The scales criterion are: » creativity, and » productivity.

TABLE 15, CONTINUED

Name and author of the tool	Objective	Number of items and scale of responses	Factors or dimensions
Creative Climate Questionnaire (CCQ: Ekvall, cited in Mathisen & Einarsen, 2004)	Assess organizational conditions that can stimulate or hinder creativity and innovation or the climate for creativity in organizations.	The instrument consists of 50 items (five items in each dimension) with four response categories (0–strongly disagree, 1–agree up to a point, 2–agree, 3–agree strongly).	It measures 10 dimensions of the climate: » challenge, » freedom, » idea support, » trust/openness, » dynamism/liveliness, » playfulness/humor, » debates, » conflicts, » risk taking, and » idea time.
Situational Outlook Questionnaire (SOQ; Isaksen, Lauer, & Ekvall, cited in Mathisen & Einarsen, 2004)	Assess organizational conditions that can stimulate or hinder creativity and innovation or climate for creativity in organizations.	The instrument consists of 50 items with four response alternatives (0–not at all applicable, 1–applicable to some extent, 2–fairly applicable, 3–applicable to a high extent).	This is a version of the CCQ translated into English with the exception of the scale "dynamism/liveliness" that was removed. A subscale called "challenge" was added.
Team Climate Inventory (TCI; Anderson & West, cited in Mathisen & Einarsen, 2004)	Assess work group climate for innovation.	Two versions: one with 61 items and another with 38 items. Different response categories: three of them with 7 points and one with 5 points.	It consists of four dimensions: » vision, » participative safety, » task orientation, and » support for innovation.

Note. Based on Mathisen and Einarsen (2004).

At the first step toward developing the instrument, we carried out an extensive review of national and international literature on the topic of creativity in organizations, and more specifically on facilitators and barriers to creativity in the workplace. Given that the tools built in other countries do not reflect the characteristics of the Brazilian context, we opted for the creation of the scale here described.

Preliminary Research

After an analysis of the literature, individual interviews were conducted with 25 professionals who, at the time of the research, worked in different kinds of organizations. Among them, 22 worked in public and three in private organizations; 19 were females and 6 were males.

The main purpose of the interview was to identify stimulants and obstacles to creativity in the workplace as perceived by different professionals. The interview included five questions:

- What are the characteristics of a workplace that promotes creativity?
- What are the characteristics of a workplace that inhibits creativity?
- What are the factors that contribute to the promotion of creativity and innovation that are present in your workplace?
- What are the factors that inhibit creativity and innovation that are present in your workplace?
- What is necessary to have a climate favorable to creativity in your workplace?

The objective of the first two questions was to identify the stimulants and barriers to creativity in any work environment, while questions 3 and 4 aimed to identify the facilitators and barriers in the organization where the interviewees worked. The final question intended to identify suggestions of actions to be implemented to promote a favorable climate for creativity in the interviewees' workplace.

The participants were introduced to the concepts of creativity and innovation in order to subsidize their answers. We adopted the perspective of Amabile and Gryskiewicz (1989), who consider creativity as the production of new and appropriate ideas, both by individuals and small groups that work in a given context. Stimulants were understood as features of the work that promote the expression of creativity, and barriers as those features that hinder such expression. The work environment included all of the factors surrounding the individual, including the people with whom the individual interacts with in that environment.

It should be stressed that the main purpose of conducting the interviews was to produce items that expressed stimulants and barriers to creativity, to be part of a quantitative instrument for data collection. The analysis of the responses obtained in the interviews resulted in 12 categories of stimulants and 13 of barriers to creativity in the workplace. An operational definition of each of these categories was made, which constituted the hypothesized factors of the instrument. Thus, the instrument originally consisted of 12 categories of stimulants and 13 categories of barriers to creativity in the workplace.

Besides examining the literature and the results of the interviews, scales developed in other countries were also analyzed. Following the recommendations of Günther (1996) and Pasquali (1997), the following criteria were taken into account in the preparation of each item:

- Construct items that express common behaviors in the workplace.
- Include statements that aimed to assess the individuals' perceptions about their work environment.
- Prepare items that only express a single idea.
- Write items that are clear and objective.
- Avoid long statements and extreme and negative expressions.
- Build a set of items that express barriers and other that indicate stimulants to creativity, according to the results of the interviews and the literature on the topic.
- Elaborate all of the items in such a way that they reflect features of the work environment of organizations.

Semantic Analysis of the Items

Up to this point, 184 items were constructed. Next, they were submitted to a semantic analysis and to judges' analysis (Pasquali, 1997). The goal of the semantic analysis was to assess the level of understanding of the items by individuals who could compose the research sample. The idea was to ensure that the items not be inadequate because they were overly simple, so that the individuals with higher educational levels did not feel interested in answering them, or so complex that individuals with lower educational levels did not feel comfortable in completing the questionnaire or did not understand the meaning of the items. For this analysis, the participants were divided into three groups consisting of three individuals and one group with two individuals, totaling 11 employees with different educational levels from a bank (institution where the instrument was validated).

Caution was taken in conducting the semantics validation among these workers. It was explained to them that the purpose was to know the understanding that they had of the items, allowing them to feel free to criticize the items, and even to suggest a better wording for them. At that time, the five-point response scale (1–strongly disagree; 2–disagree somewhat; 3–not sure; 4–slightly agree; 5–strongly agree) was also presented to the groups.

Judges' Analysis

In the process of developing an instrument, it is not enough to check if the items are understandable and appropriate to the intended audience; developers must also ensure that they measure what they intend to measure. Thus, Pasquali (1997) recommended analysis of the items by judges in order to verify the behavioral adequacy of the latent attributes in the items. The ideal is to consult with various experts in the subject matter for this type of analysis. However, on the occasion of the research, it was only possible to have an expert on creativity. Thus, several readings were made of each item conducting the necessary adjustments (inclusion, exclusion, and adaptation of items). A total of 142 items were obtained after these preliminary steps of the instrument validation.

Version of the Questionnaire Before the Statistical Validation

The questionnaire was structured in three parts. The cover contained the initial information about the objective of the research, the presentation of the researcher with her institutional affiliation, general instructions about how to respond to the questionnaire (preserving the anonymity of respondents), the guidelines on how to return the completed questionnaire, and collaboration acknowledgements. This part of the questionnaire should be adapted in future applications in order to characterize the research and identify the researcher.

The first part contained the 142 items related to stimulants and barriers to creativity in the workplace. These items were mixed, so that the respondent did not know if they were stimulants or barriers. The second part included five questions asking the participants to make a general assessment of the environment where they work in relation to creativity. The purpose was to verify the convergent validity of the scale, by means of the calculation of correlations between the items of stimulants and barriers and these overall evaluation items (see Figure 9).

This part is not necessary in future applications, except to revalidate the instrument when the researcher wants to verify the convergent validity.

The third part included several demographic variables, needed to characterize the participants, as well as to conduct correlation and regression analyses to ascertain possible predictors of stimulants and barriers to creativity in the workplace. For future applications, the researcher must include the variables considered important for the study in question, adapting this part of the questionnaire as needed.

Statistical Validation

The sample consisted of 1,003 employees of a large state bank in Brazil. The Statistical Package for Social Sciences (SPSS) was used. After the sample analysis for missing data, and the extreme uni- and multivariate cases (outliers), 10 cases were excluded and 993 cases remained to be subjected to statistical validation (factor analysis and reliability). The ratio of cases per variable was 7.14 to 1 which, according to Tabachnick and Fidell (1996), constitutes an adequate sample for factor analysis considering the size (more than 300 cases) and the ratio between cases and questions (a minimum of five cases per variable).

Exploratory analyses were conducted and it was verified that all assumptions for factor analysis were met. Three items were deleted because they had large asymmetry that affected the factor analysis. Next, we proceeded to estimate the factors, with the method of "principal components"—with the remaining 139 items and 12 factors estimated. Factor analysis was performed by the extraction process "Principal Axis Factoring" (PAF), oblique rotation, with 12 factors, and with higher and lower number of factors, in order to determine the best factor solution for the instrument.

Names were assigned to factors according to their component items, prioritizing the highest load factor and based on the theoretical framework regarding creativity in organizations. The factors, their component items, and the main statistical indices are described in the following section.

The following items were used:	
a. The section where I work is characterized by creativity.	( ) No ( ) Sometimes ( ) Yes
b. The section where I work is characterized by innovation.	( ) No ( ) Sometimes ( ) Yes
c. My organization is characterized by creativity.	( ) No ( ) Sometimes ( ) Yes
d. My organization is characterized by innovation.	( ) No ( ) Sometimes ( ) Yes
e. My workplace offers the necessary conditions for the expression of my creative potential.	( ) always ( ) very rarely ( ) almost always ( ) never ( ) sometimes

FIGURE 9. *Evaluation items.*

Factors, Items' Description, Variance, and Cronbach's Alpha of Each Factor

The criteria for retention of items in the factors were *eigenvalue* equal to or greater than 1.5, factor loadings of the items equal to or greater than .30, and similarity of content of the items. After factor analysis and internal consistency analysis of the factors (Cronbach's Alpha), 12 factors, eight stimulants, and four barriers to creativity were extracted, including 97 items.

In Appendix D, the items are arranged in their respective factors, already with suggested numbering, in order to mix them in the composition of the instrument. The numbering in the tables below and from now on in this text refers to the suggestion to the composition of the questionnaire for future applications. Thus, the items are numbered from 1 to 97.

It should be pointed out that 10 items were loaded in more than one factor (items 5, 9, 40, 44, 60, 66, 70, 72, 77, and 83). They are called complex items. We decided to keep them in the instrument, to be improved in future revalidation and be evaluated on their relevance to a single factor or exclusion. Of the 12 factors extracted by factor analysis, eight factors represent stimulants to creativity and four express creativity barriers in the workplace. Initially we will describe the factors of stimulants, then those of barriers.

Using factor analysis, the factors received numbers from 1 to 12, according to the extraction. To facilitate the understanding and use in future applications, in this chapter, the factors were numbered, so that the first eight refer to stimulants (see Table 16) and the last four to barriers to creativity in the workplace environment (see Table 17).

Of the items that comprise the Appropriate Physical Environment factor, five presented positive factor loadings and five had negative factor loadings, indicating both aspects of the physical environment, respectively, that interfered with creativity at work.

Of the nine items that comprise the Positive Social Climate Among Colleagues factor, four had positive factor loadings and five were negative, thus revealing aspects of favorable and unfavorable climate for creativity in the workplace.

The Incentives to New Ideas factor contains eight items with positive factor loadings and one with negative. Such a polarization indicates the presence of items that represent incentives, stimulants, and opportunities for the development of new ideas in the workplace and an item that expresses the lack of opportunity for such an occurrence, as a function of their immediate supervisors.

Of the 10 items from the Freedom of Action factor, eight indicated a lack of freedom of action by punishing mistakes and the feeling of being watched, resulting from the negative loadings of these items. On the other hand, two positive items express the freedom of action in the workplace, whether between colleagues or boss-employee relationship.

All six items of the Challenging Activities factor have positive factor loadings and, therefore, indicate the perception of work as a challenge.

Seven items from the Adequate Salaries and Benefits factor had positive loadings considering salary and personal development programs and rewards as favorable aspects of creativity, alongside one negative item, which expressed dissatisfaction with the policy of promotion as something unfavorable in the workplace.

All 13 items comprising the factor labeled Actions by Managers and the Organization in Support of New Ideas have a positive loading and refer to managers' incentive to propose new ideas and innovative solutions to problems at work, the clarity of organizational goals, and organization of meetings as an incentive to new ideas in the workplace.

TABLE 16

Stimulants to Creativity in the Workplace

Factors	Factor items	Alpha	No. of items	% of total variance	% of common variance
Factor 1 – Appropriate physical environment	4, 8, 9, 15, 29, 40, 47, 51, 83, 87	.76	10	3.1	7.54
Factor 2 – Positive social climate among work colleagues	10, 28, 55, 57, 58, 60, 66, 68, 85	.83	9	2.4	5.84
Factor 3 – Incentive to new ideas	5, 14, 19, 35, 52, 70, 77, 80, 82	.86	9	1.9	4.62
Factor 4 – Freedom of action	1, 16, 18, 25, 34, 38, 44, 49, 89, 90	.85	10	1.7	4.14
Factor 5 – Challenging activities	12, 24, 72, 88, 93, 96	.69	6	1.5	3.65
Factor 6 – Adequate salaries and benefits	13, 17, 32, 42, 45, 62, 81, 86	.75	8	1.4	3.41
Factor 7 – Actions by managers and the organization in support of new ideas	2, 3, 5, 6, 27, 30, 41, 44, 50, 63, 70, 77, 84	.88	13	1.2	2.92
Factor 8 – Availability of material resources	9, 40, 74, 83	.68	4	1.2	2.92

TABLE 17
Barriers to Creativity in the Workplace

Factors	Factor items	Alpha	No. of items	% of total variance	% of common variance
Factor 1–Blocking of new ideas	53, 60, 61, 64, 66, 67, 76	.82	7	20.2	49.15
Factor 2–Excessive number of tasks and scarcity of time	11, 21, 31, 36, 48, 65, 72, 73, 79, 95, 97	.80	11	4.1	9.98
Factor 3–Resistance to new ideas	7, 20, 22, 23, 26, 33, 37, 39	.79	8	1.3	3.16
Factor 4–Organizational problems	43, 46, 54, 56, 59, 69, 71, 75, 78, 91, 92, 94	.70	12	1.1	2.68

The Availability of Material Resources factor is composed of three items with positive factor loadings and one with negative factor loading, indicating the presence or absence of material resources and equipment in the workplace, respectively.

The four factors of barriers to creativity with their respective indices are presented in Table 17.

The Blocking of New Ideas supervisor factor is unipolar, so that all factor loadings of the seven items are positive. They highlight the actions of managers and colleagues to block new ideas at work.

In the Excessive Number of Tasks and Scarcity of Time factor, nine items indicate lack of time and excess of service hampering creativity, and two items indicate that the organization offers the time and staff needed to develop new ideas.

The Resistance to New Ideas factor consists of eight items with negative loadings that reflect the accommodation of the supervisors and other employees, political problems, and resistance from older workers that hinder the emergence of new ideas.

The last factor that represents barriers to creativity in the workplace, labeled Organizational Problems, contains 12 items, all indicating the organizational characteristics that negatively affect the expression of new ideas in the workplace.

After statistical validation, the instrument was called Indicators of Climate for Creativity (ICC). The ICC considers aspects of different natures related to the work environment, namely:

- features of the physical environment;
- aspects related to the structure and organizational culture;
- interpersonal aspects, especially those related to receptivity and to incentives of new ideas at work; and
- features of the task.

At the time of the validation of the ICC, regression analysis was performed between the factors that compose the instrument and demographic variables, such as sex, age, whether or not the employees were in management positions, etc. The variable "management" was the best predictor of a greater number of factors from the ICC. The managers tended to perceive the environment in which they worked with greater presence of stimulants to creativity than barriers. This result demonstrates the importance of including workers in different segments and functions in an organization in order to know the conditions for creativity in the workplace.

Fonseca (2001) administered the ICC to 750 employees at the same bank in which the instrument was validated previously (Bruno-Faria, 1996), with the main objective to identify relationships between organizational commitment, stimulants and obstacles to creativity, and the performance of 42 teams at work. The author applied only the ICC scales that showed higher levels of internal reliability. Among other results, it was observed that performance of higher levels was linked to the perception of low index of barriers and high index of stimulants to creativity in the workplace. The main predictor of perceived team performance at work identified by Fonseca (2001) was the scale of stimulant to creativity labeled Actions by Managers and the Organization in Support of New Ideas, responsible for 42% of the total variance.

Final Considerations

The validation study resulted in an instrument consisting of eight scales of stimulants and four barriers to creativity in the workplace, with 97 items (see Appendix D: Indicators of the Climate for Creativity in the Workplace). Taking into account the alpha internal-consistency of each factor and the factor loadings, the factors of stimulants to creativity (2, 3, 4, and 7) and those of barriers to creativity (1, 2, and 3) were considered strong (an alpha Cronbach greater than .79); two factors of stimulants (1 and 6) were evaluated as promising; and two factors of stimulants (5 and 8) and factor 4 of barriers to creativity as weak. These results highlight the need of new studies with the instrument to confirm its factor structure.

Nowadays, the ICC is being reformulated in order to adapt language and to include and exclude items to bring them to the current reality of organizations. Nevertheless, the instrument, described in this chapter, has good psychometric qualities and can be applied in different organizations. It is suggested that each alteration made to ICC be held to new factor analysis and internal consistency in order to ascertain the pertinence of items in the factors. It is hoped that this instrument may provide the basis for future studies about creativity in the organizational context, as well as for the management of creativity in the workplace.

CHAPTER 7

STRATEGIES FOR CREATING AT WORK*

Melissa Machado de Moraes and Suzana Maria Valle Lima

In the last two decades, changes in work contexts and settings have emerged as a recurrent theme for organizational behavior and management scholars. The concern with performance has migrated from sole efficiency to an inclusion of effectiveness in order to sustain organizational survival, which is now attributed to the ability to maintain internal coherence and consistency with the environment, despite its turbulence (Silva, 2003). This ability requires models and management approaches that are guided by freedom, flexibility, creativity, and innovation.

When analyzing Brazilian research on organizational behavior from 1996 to 2004 (Borges-Andrade, Coelho, & Queiroga, 2006), the low participation (2%) of the theme *creativity* in this production is clear. In contrast, 14% of the

---

* The construct referred to was formerly known as "Creative Strategies at Work." The researchers chose to change the English denomination to "Strategies for Creating at Work" to better convey the underlying phenomena.

publications analyzed focused on organizational change, while another 16% focused on related topics such as learning and culture, sometimes used interchangeably with organizational change (Lima, 2003). The shortfall in national production, therefore, is specific to research on creativity in the workplace.

Alencar and Fleith (2003c) pointed out that the focus on individual, social, cultural, and historical interactions observed more recently in international research has been poorly covered in Brazilian studies on creativity. This approach seems to better encompass the complexity of the phenomenon of creativity in the workplace (Bruno-Faria, 2004), facilitating its understanding while establishing the foundations for future interventions. From this point of view, investigation of psychological processes underlying creative behavior should consider proximal and specific antecedents, which could also play an intervening role. According to Amabile (1997), contextual aspects affect creativity by means of their influence on individual aspects, especially intrinsic task motivation. Commenting on Amabile's model, Alencar and Fleith (2003c) reaffirmed that individuals feel more motivated when the activity is challenging and interests them, thus facilitating greater involvement.

A motivational construct in particular—creative self-efficacy—has been presented as a mediator between individual/contextual aspects and creative performance (e.g., Choi, 2004; Tierney & Farmer, 2004). This mediating effect is consistent with results from other research on self-efficacy (e.g., Ambrose & Kulik, 1999; Eccles & Wigfield, 2002; Latham & Pinder, 2005) and with Amabile's model (1997). Self-efficacy beliefs refer to one's perceptions about his or her ability to mobilize affective, cognitive, and motivational resources—in addition to behavior—in order to control events in their lives. More specifically, it is the beliefs in one's capabilities to organize and execute courses of action needed to produce given attainments (Bandura, 1982; Pajares, 2004). This definition conveys a gap between creative performance and creative self-efficacy, in which the mobilization of various resources takes place. Within this gap lies the space to be occupied by the conceptual proposition of strategies for creating at work (Moraes, 2006), presented in more detail in the next section.

Strategies for Creating at Work: Concept Characterization

The characterization of strategies for creating at work was carried out from an analogy with the concept of learning strategies. This section focuses on the proximity between learning and creativity, explaining the usefulness of the analogy adopted. Following, a summary of the literature on learning strategies at work is presented, in which its theoretical and empirical structure is described, and considerations of its relevance are put forward. Finally, the concept of strategies for creating at work is established, as well as the initial basis for its investigation.

Learning and Creating Affinity

Creativity is sometimes seen as a quality of individuals capable of creative acts, other times as a quality of the outcomes of these acts. More often, creativity is seen as a process that generates such outcomes. Although there is reasonable variation in the concepts of creativity, there is agreement in terms of its usual constituents: Utility and novelty are attributes often associated with creative ideas (Alencar & Fleith, 2003b; Bruno-Faria, 2003, 2004; Runco, 2004).

There are several definitions for learning in psychology, but generally it refers to enduring changes in individual behavior resulting from its interaction with the context and not merely the result of the natural process of aging (Abbad & Borges-Andrade, 2004). Just as there are multiple definitions of learning, there are also different kinds of learning. Seen in more detail, the contents of some taxonomies of learning objectives regarding the cognitive domain reveal the points at which the phenomena of learning and creating resemble each other. In virtually all of these taxonomies, learning at more complex levels is very similar to creative behavior, requiring the learner to produce something new and emphasizing the uniqueness and originality of its action (Abbad & Borges-Andrade, 2004; Reigeluth & Moore, 1999). These affinities between the two phenomena led to the use of the concept of learning strategies in the initial conception of creative strategies at work.

Learning strategies refer to efforts in which individuals engage to learn. These efforts may be intentional, selected and controlled by the learner, or their use can be automated, which would free up capacity for other mental activities. The strategies may be restricted to certain domains or valid for a wide variety of situations. In the learning process, individuals necessarily engage in one or more strategies, since they are often essential to learning, but it is reasonable to assume that there are individual differences regarding the nature of the strategies used (Warr & Allan, 1998).

At the organizational level, Warr and Allan (1998) originally suggested a structure composed of nine strategies for learning at work, containing two distinct types: primary strategies, which are used when there is direct engagement with the content being learned; and support strategies, composed of self-regulation procedures that impact learning indirectly. Primary strategies can be cognitive (reproduction, organization, and elaboration of material to be learned) or behavioral (practical application, seeking help from written material, and interpersonal help seeking). Support or self-regulation strategies involve efforts directed at emotion control, motivation control, and comprehension monitoring.

There is partial support for the structure just described, in both the international literature (Holman, Epitropaki, & Fernie, 2001; Warr & Downing, 2000) and in Brazilian research on learning strategies in different contexts (Lopes-Ribeiro, 2005; Pantoja, 2004; Zerbini, 2003). Results from factor analysis approximate the proposed structure; nonetheless, there is an important factor reorganization in some of these studies, including the formation of factors mixing cognitive and behavioral aspects.

The importance of learning strategies stems from evidence suggesting the relationship between use of strategies and learning outcomes, and between training on learning strategies and learning outcomes, as well as the interaction of learning strategies with individual characteristics in explaining learning outcomes (Pantoja, 2004; Warr & Allan, 1998; Warr & Downing, 2000).

Strategies for Creating at Work: A New Concept

The proposed definition of strategies for creating at work involves cognitive, behavioral, and self-regulation strategies, similar to learning strategies. Strategies for creating at work refer to efforts made by individuals to favor the creation of new and useful ideas in solving work problems. They may be mental processes in which individuals engage, manifested behaviors, or self-regulatory actions aimed at facilitating the process of creative problem solving at work (Moraes, 2006).

Strategies for creating at work are actions that facilitate: (a) the identification and understanding of work problems; (b) preparation for solving these problems; (c) the emergence of the idea or solution sought out; and, finally, (d) the assessment of the validity and usefulness of the proposed idea and its improvement. The underlying assumption is that the creative process in organizations always involves problem solving, even when these problems are not explicit at first (Moraes, 2006).

It is reasonable to assume proximity between creative strategies and cognitive styles, especially when considering measures of creative styles, styles of creative problem solving and the like (e.g., Creative Problem Solving Profile [CPSP], in Puccio, 1999; Foursight Cognitive Style Inventory in Puccio, Wheeler & Cassander, 2004; Kirton Adaptation-Innovation Inventory [KAI], and VIEW: Assessment of Problem Solving Style, both in Selby, Treffinger, Isaksen & Lauer, 2004; Styles of Thinking and Creating, in Wechsler, 2006a). This similarity is also found in the learning literature, and conceptual redundancy may occur when style is defined as preferred strategies.

Strategies for creating at work are *not* tools or techniques taught through instruction or learned from textbooks about creative problem solving, although the individual may also make use of these to promote creative problem solving. Even though they can be formally taught, strategies for creating at work stem from previous individual experiences, from cognitive abilities, from natural learning, and other aspects that may be involved in the search for resolution of work problems (either existing problems or new problems identified in the creative process). These strategies should, therefore, be flexible, and vary according to the context in which they are applied and the domain which is involved. Such flexibility is similar to what is observed in learning strategies (Pantoja, 2004; Warr & Allan, 1998) and in the creative process (Runco, 2004). These characteristics of strategies for creating at work would help explain individual–context interaction and creative performance at work itself.

Despite the use of learning strategies at work as an analogous concept, it is not assumed that the theoretical structure of strategies for creating at work is similar or divergent from the structure of learning strategies. The understanding is that there is insufficient evidence in the literature on creativity concerning this issue, in the manner proposed here, to assume a specific theoretical structure. Likewise, Brazilian measures of learning strategies at work point to differing arrangements, also failing to provide the basis to hypothesize such structure. These considerations about the conceptual nature of strategies for creating at work are the foundations for the measure development described in detail in the next section.

Strategies for Creating at Work: Measure Development

In this section the method used to carry out the measure development is described, followed by the presentation of results obtained and a discussion of these results. First, the sample, data collection process, and the measure construction are characterized. Subsequently, the procedures used in data analysis are summarized, including the extraction and rotation of factors, the measures of internal consistency and homogeneity, the exploration of facets and second order factors, and further exploration of the validated measure. Finally, the results of this study are discussed taking into account the initial theoretical proposition and the literature supporting it.

Method

The data for this study were collected in a public sector organization, based in Brasilia with regional branches in nine Brazilian capitals. The staff in this organization at the time of data collection was composed of 4,597 permanent employees and 1,593 temporary workers, trainees, and apprentices, all of whom were invited to respond to the survey. From their responses, 878 completed surveys were obtained. The exclusion of missing data and outliers resulted in a database containing 688 observations. The sample was composed mostly of permanent employees (95%), men (76%), with a graduate degree (57%), more than 50 years of age (49%), and 20 years within the company (47%). Most of the participants were trained in applied social sciences and engineering, specifically in management/accounting (26.89%) and economics (19.04%), with the majority (62%)

at least partially working in their field of formal training. Considering the prevalence of permanent employees' responses, there is congruence between the sample profile and population characteristics.

Data were collected via an electronic form hosted on a special Internet site contracted for this purpose, after an invitation to all permanent and temporary employees was sent out to their corporate electronic address. This message included an invitation to participate in the research, as well as the link to the electronic form and information about the research content. Twelve days after the first invitation a second one was sent out, in order to ensure enough responses to perform the statistical analysis. As usual in this type of data collection, peaks of responses were concentrated in the first 3 days after both invitations were sent out, dramatically reducing in subsequent days and ceasing completely after 10 days.

The measure of strategies for creating at work was constructed in three stages. The initial step consisted of reviewing the literature, identifying related measures, and evaluating existing ones (Pantoja, 2004; Warr & Downing, 2000), to allow concept operationalization. This step resulted in the formulation of 92 items, which were submitted to content validation by experts to verify their theoretical relevance. This validation occurred in conjunction with the validation of other measures in construction by the researchers: creative self-efficacy at work, work motivation and socio-psychological context for innovation. The process was conducted by five experts, four Ph.D.s and a graduate student in psychology, with a two-way table asking for the judge to point out the relationship of each item with the concepts being validated. Additionally, each expert was asked to assess the clarity of items, using a scale from 1 ("no clarity") to 4 ("total clarity"). Those items with an agreement score equal or superior to 80% (regarding the measured concept) and a score (arithmetic mean) of at least 3.40 concerning clarity were kept in the instrument. This adjustment step resulted in 66 items of strategies for creating at work.

The third step was the semantic validation of items to ensure that they were comprehensible to the audience. We invited three employees with different roles and levels of education in the target organization to apply the scale in its first version. These employees were monitored individually in a simulated reply to the survey, conducted at his or her work desk. To do so, an e-mail address of the survey was provided and participants were asked to inform whenever they had any difficulty or discomfort replying to items in the survey or browsing the electronic form, which already consisted of a full version of the survey, including sociodemographic questions. This approach also allowed checking accessibility of the host website and research instrument, as well as the understanding of the survey in its final form.

Following the suggestions offered in this step, a few semantic adjustments were made, especially in sociodemographic items, and three items of strategies for creating at work were excluded for being redundant. The final version of the survey, therefore, had 63 items of strategies for creating at work, to be answered in a 10-point scale, anchored at its extremes (1 "never," 10 "always"), and 11 sociodemographic questions.

Additionally, the survey also contained seven items of creative self-efficacy at work (Moraes, 2006), to be answered on a 10-point confidence scale, with anchors at the extreme (1 "I cannot in any way," 10 "I am very certain I can"). This joint application of creative self-efficacy and strategies for creating at work made possible the assessment of the discriminant validity to better support the proposed measure.

The data analysis involved exploratory factor analysis of the strategies for creating at work variable set, examination of internal consistency and homogeneity of factors, and assessment of discriminant validity, as well as an additional analysis of the relationship between strategies for creating at work and the sociodemographic aspects measured. Given the relevance of these procedures for the development and validation of the measure, they require exploration in more detail, presented in the next section.

Results

The exploratory analysis of data showed a low incidence of dropouts, which entailed the removal of 25 cases with more than 10% of the questions left blank. Strategies for creating at work items had only a few missing data, with less than 1.3% per variable. Initial visual inspection of the distribution curves of continuous variables, and assessment of their levels of skewness and kurtosis denoted a slight negative asymmetry (up to -1.25) at levels that would not affect the analysis. Investigation of extreme cases showed 58 possible extreme univariate cases and 107 multivariate extreme cases, which were removed.

The database used for the factor analysis thus had 688 observations, ensuring the proportion of 10.92 subjects per item. The factorability of the correlation matrix was examined from the size and prevalence of correlations and the value of its determinant, which approached zero. The adequacy index of Kaiser Meyer Olkein sample obtained also demonstrated the feasibility of factor analysis.

Following this, the number of factors to be extracted was defined, a crucial decision in measure development according to Zwick and Velicer (1986). The K1 criterion suggests retaining factors with an *eigenvalue* above one, which would entail the extraction of 11 factors. Another commonly used criterion is visual inspection of the scree plot, which in this case points to the extraction of six factors. However, Zwick and Velicer indicated the risk of overextraction such criteria entails and recommended the use of parallel analysis, a much more accurate method. The comparison of randomly obtained *eigenvalues* and the empirical *eigenvalues* from the sample indicated the extraction of six factors.

The next step was the extraction of these factors, using principal axis factoring method and direct oblimin oblique rotation. Of the 63 initial items, 46 were maintained, 12 were cut because they were low-loading items (factor loading less than .32) or complex (loadings greater than .32 on more than one factor), and five items were cut for not completely adhering theoretically to the assigned factor—and such exclusion enhanced factor reliability. After the removal of several items, it is recommended to perform a new factor analysis, following usual procedure in measure construction (Clark & Watson, 1995; Costello & Osborne, 2005; Laros, 2004; Tabachnick & Fidell, 2001).

The final exploratory analysis involved a new round of principal component analysis, verification of the factorability of the correlation matrix, and definition of the number of factors to extract. Although six factor extraction was again indicated by the scree plot and parallel analysis, the researchers chose to extract five factors, because the initial exploratory factor analysis produced one factor with only two items ("I avoid being distracted by other tasks when I'm trying to solve a problem at work" and "When investigating a problem at work, I leave aside other matters to focus only on it"), one of which was excluded for having a factor loading below .32. This result, indeed, is compatible with Zwick and Velicer's (1986) indication that the parallel analysis criterion sometimes suggests the retention of weak components.

Also dismissed in the final factor analysis was an item that had migrated from one factor to another to which it did not adhere theoretically ("At work, I generate new ideas from the suggestions of my colleagues"), with similar factor loadings in both factors (.31 and .33). Its exclusion did not affect the reliability of the factor. The final factor solution is presented in detail below.

Internal Consistency and Factors Homogeneity

The final factor solution contains 44 items distributed in five factors explaining 50.02% of the variance observed before the rotation and with Cronbach alphas varying between .75 and .95. The average correlation between items recorded in the factors, in turn, varies between .266 and .513 and its variance between .006 and .009, satisfactory values considering Clark and Watson's (1995) recommendation that such average should lie within .15 and .50 and have limited variance.

The empirical structure of the first factor is represented in Table 18, with the description of its 19 items and their respective factor loadings and communalities. Analyzing the content of the items, one finds cognitive strategies related to generating ideas and solving problems at work, such as association of perspectives, diversification of ideas, reformulation of problems, and extrinsic evaluation. The underlying component of these items is thought flexibility, which allows looking at the same issue in varying ways. Thus, this factor was called "Flexible Thinking."

Table 19 presents the empirical structure of the second factor, containing its eight items and their factor loadings and communalities. In this factor there are cognitive strategies related to the exploration of unusual alternatives, including fantasy and suspension of judgment, used in the pursuit of problem solving and idea generation at work. There are also self-regulatory strategies that help to maintain focus, effort, and motivation involved in this operation. This factor was called "Imagination and Introspection," as these seem to be the binding elements that characterize most of its items.

The third factor is reported in Table 20, which shows its empirical structure, the five constituent items and their factor loadings and communalities. Items in this factor are related to self-regulation strategies of emotional control, intended to minimize or prevent anxiety and frustration inherent in problem solving and generation of ideas at work. It was thus named "Emotional Control."

The fourth factor, whose empirical structure can be seen in Table 21, was named "Inspiring Reading," for all four items reflect behavioral strategies related to reading or looking for reading material in order to promote problem solving and idea generation at work.

TABLE 18

Flexible Thinking (Factor 1)

Item	Content	Load	h²
20	To solve a problem at work I try to combine different ideas.	.77	.67
22	I seek to understand a work problem from different angles.	.74	.67
28	I combine different perspectives in generating ideas about my work.	.69	.69
6	I reflect on how to best implement an idea about work.	.67	.53
8	When I have an idea at work, I often wonder what would be its consequences on other activities in my sector.	.64	.54
7	Even after I have mastered a work subject, I strive to see it in new ways.	.64	.52
4	When analyzing a problem at work, I think about how I might redefine it.	.61	.47
34	I put together different ideas to solve work problems.	.60	.68
30	I think about many different ways to accomplish a task at work.	.59	.60
3	When I reflect on solutions to a problem, I think how they would affect other areas of my work.	.59	.53
26	I use many approaches to reflect about a work topic.	.58	.63
19	I refine the ideas I have at work, improving proposed solutions.	.58	.63
11	To better understand a work problem, I try to collect information from various sources.	.56	.58
33	I try to reformulate a work problem to better understand it.	.54	.55
24	I evaluate the usefulness of the solutions I find for a work problem.	.53	.61
44	I seek to create many alternative solutions to a problem.	.53	.50
1	To express my opinion on a work issue that I gather varied information about it.	.51	.47
14	For work, I consider the most diverse ideas that come to mind, even if they may seem inappropriate at first.	.48	.49
2	I make a mental list of possible solutions to a problem at work.	.43	.37
Cronbach's alpha (α) .95		19 items	
Average correlation between items .481		Variance .006	

TABLE 19

Imagination and Introspection (Factor 2)

Item	Content	Load	h^2
25	To break the routine, I do my work in ways I am not accustomed to.	.53	.37
23	I play in my head with bizarre and unusual ideas about my work.	.49	.46
41	I seek an isolated environment in order to focus only on the work problem I am analyzing.	.45	.25
16	To have different ideas at work, I pretend to know nothing about a subject.	.44	.39
17	I imagine the perfect solution to a problem at work, even if it is fantastical.	.43	.40
29	When I try to resolve an issue at work I contemplate it for extended periods of time.	.42	.37
38	When reflecting on possible solutions to a problem at work, I leave my criticism for later.	.38	.19
43	I talk to myself mentally, encouraging myself to be creative at work.	.32	.35
	Cronbach's alpha (α) .75	8 items	
	Average correlation between items .266	Variance .006	

TABLE 20

Emotional Control (Factor 3)

Item	Content	Load	h^2
21	When I cannot solve a work problem, I temporarily distract myself with other matters.	.70	.47
15	When I cannot find a solution to a problem at work, I "give it a rest."	.67	.43
10	When anxiety stops me from having ideas at work, I try to relax and think about good things.	.59	.50
12	At work, I intercalate moments of intense activity in problem solving with moments of fun and relaxation.	.57	.35
5	When I am pressed for ideas at work, I seek ways to reduce the pressure.	.43	.39
	Cronbach's alpha (α) .76	5 items	
	Average correlation between items .389	Variance .009	

TABLE 21

Inspiring Reading (Factor 4)

Item	Content	Load	h^2
13	To have ideas at work, I keep myself updated by reading articles and texts about my area of expertise.	.74	.57
9	I read up on several topics to inspire me to have new ideas about work.	.58	.57
27	I seek reading material on the work problem that I have to solve.	.58	.55
18	I select the best sources of information about my activities, so I can access them when I have problems at work.	.45	.51
	Cronbach's alpha (α) .81	4 items	
	Average correlation between items .513	Variance .008	

The fifth factor has its empirical structure reproduced in Table 22, presenting its eight items and their factor loadings and communalities. The items depicted in this factor are behavioral strategies of interpersonal help seeking used to solve problems at work. This includes items that reflect the flexibility that would facilitate such interaction. It also has cognitive strategies related to the use of analogies in understanding and solving work problems. This factor was called "Interaction and Analogy."

Exploration of Facets and of Higher Order Factors

In some of the factors extracted, a subset of items that deal with related albeit distinct theoretical dimensions could be identified. The existence of facets was considered, since its presence is not uncommon in instruments that aim to measure complex psychological phenomena. This is a result of heterogeneous factors whose items are organized in groups with greater homogeneity among themselves, representing specific aspects of the phenomenon. To explore this possibility, the same steps above were performed, including principal component analysis to assess the factorability of the variable set, extraction of factors by principal axis, and oblique rotation. This procedure identified two facets in the "Flexible Thinking" factor, presented in Table 23.

The first facet is composed of 14 items dealing with association of perspectives, diversification of ideas, and reframing problems; it is therefore

TABLE 22

Interaction and Analogy (Factor 5)

Item	Content	Load	h²
36	When I have a work problem to solve, I seek help from more experienced colleagues.	.68	.50
37	To better understand new situations at work, I look for things that are familiar to me.	.56	.45
42	I discuss the problem I'm solving with my coworkers.	.55	.51
32	I check whether the methods that I know apply to solving new problems at work.	.54	.57
31	I talk about work problems with people with interests similar to mine.	.50	.48
40	I recognize the limitations of my own ideas about my work.	.47	.28
39	To better understand my tasks, I compare them with previous work experiences.	.44	.42
35	When analyzing a work problem, if necessary, I will change my initial opinion.	.41	.40
	Cronbach's alpha (α) .84	8 items	
	Average correlation between items .394	Variance .007	

called "Integration and Variety." The second facet, called "Solutions and Effects," contained five items that deal with reasoning about elements external to ideas and solutions, like potential consequences, implementation options, and ways to speak up about these ideas and solutions.

Additionally, the existence of a second order factor was explored, in view of the prevalence of moderate correlations among the first order factors. For this purpose the first order factors were used as study variables (Floyd & Widaman, 1995), using the unweighted factor scores of each respondent (Laros, 2004). We then repeated the factor analytic procedures and obtained a single factor called Strategies for Creating at Work (α = .79), which explains 57.20% of total observed variance and has an *eigenvalue* equal to 2.86.

The exploration of a hierarchical solution that adequately represents the phenomenon under investigation was based on the Floyd and Widaman

TABLE 23

Facets of Flexible Thinking

Content	Facet 1 Integration & Variety Load	Facet 2 Solutions & Effects Load
I combine different perspectives in generating ideas about my work.	.92	
I put together different ideas to solve work problems.	.88	
I use many approaches to reflect about a work topic.	.81	
I seek to understand a work problem from different angles.	.80	
To solve a problem at work I try to combine different ideas.	.79	
I evaluate the usefulness of the solutions that I find for a work problem.	.70	
I think about many different ways to accomplish a task at work.	.68	
I try to reformulate a work problem to better understand it.	.63	
I refine the ideas I have at work, improving proposed solutions.	.62	
For work, I consider the most diverse ideas that come into my mind, even though they may seem inappropriate at first.	.59	
To better understand a work problem, I try to collect information from various sources.	.59	
I seek to create many alternative solutions to a problem.	.56	
Even after I have mastered a work subject, I strive to see it in new ways.	.38	
When analyzing a problem at work, I think about how I might redefine it.	.37	
When I reflect on solutions to a problem, I think about how they would affect other areas of my work.		.78
To express my opinion on a work issue, I gather varied information about it.		.69
I make a mental list of possible solutions to a problem at work .		.59
When I have an idea at work, I often wonder what would be its consequences for other activities in my sector.		.54
I reflect on how to best implement an idea about work.		.49
Cronbach's alpha (α)	.94	.82
Number of items	14	5
Average correlation between items	.516	.473
Variance	.006	.005

(1995) argument that "hierarchical solutions are probably appropriate for many psychological instruments, because most psychological constructs consists of correlated multiple facets" (p. 293). Smith and McCarthy (1995) also considered the identification of higher order factors and facets as essential to measure construction and refinement, and pointed out that the procedure is underused. Figure 10 graphically represents the hierarchical solution found in the exploratory factor analysis conducted, including in it the facets, the first order factors, and general factor obtained (see the final version of the measure in the Appendix E).

Additional Exploration of the Validated Measure

The measure of strategies for creating at work was applied simultaneously to a measure of creative self-efficacy at work (Moraes, 2006). Although the literature indicates probable relationship between the concepts, such measures must be distinguished clearly, demonstrating discriminant validity. Following the recommendation of Clark and Watson (1995), an exploratory factor analysis containing all items on both measures was made: 44 items regarding strategies for creating at work, and seven items of creative self-efficacy at work. The same steps were conducted as previously with this set of 51 items, and the resulting empirical structure unequivocally maintained the original factors of strategies for creating at work, clearly demonstrating the appropriateness of the factor solution proposed. Creative self-efficacy average correlation ($r = .37$) with the first-order factors of strategies for creating at work was low to moderate, varying from $r = .18$ (Imagination and Introspection) to $r = .60$ (Flexible Thinking).

This measure exploration also entailed analyzing relationships with sociodemographic data, keeping in mind the caveats mentioned by Costello and Osborne (2005) regarding the use of essentially exploratory procedures for inferential calculations.

The independent variables used were: working in the same area of formal training, level of education, type of current job position, age, time within the company, and time within the current job position. On this chapter only the significant differences in average verified by post hoc Tukey method ($p < .05$) are reported in Table 24. Complete results are available for consultation upon request to the researchers. In carrying out these ANOVAs, the Levene test was computed ($p > .05$) demonstrating homogeneity of variances, a requirement which, if violated, would invalidate this calculation (Moore, 2000). The only exceptions were the groups'

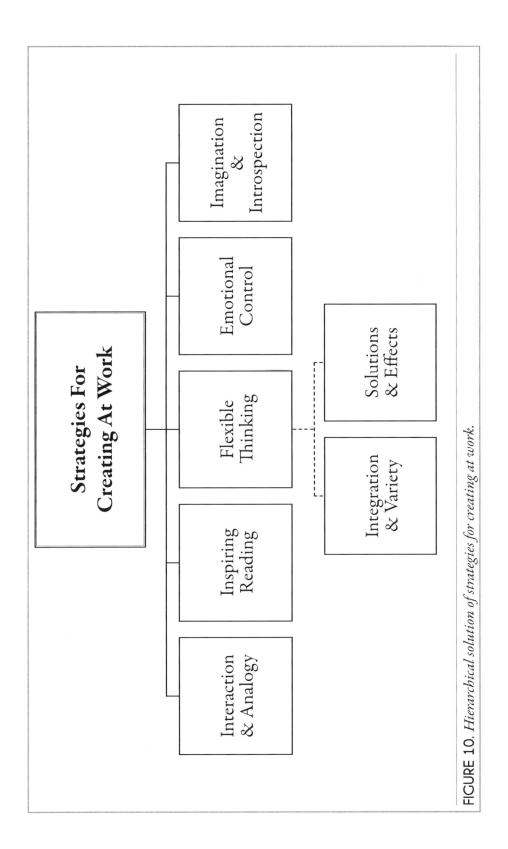

FIGURE 10. *Hierarchical solution of strategies for creating at work.*

TABLE 24

Significant Differences Between Factor Scores: Strategies for Creating at Work

Factor	Variable	Groups	Mean differences	*p*
Imagination and Introspection	Position	Administrative Support > Manager	1.03	.020
	Age	50 to 59 years > 30 to 39 years	.65	.0001
		50 to 59 years > 40 to 49 years	.42	.009
	Time in the Company	From 26 to 30 years > From 6 to 10 years	.61	.002
		From 26 to 30 years > 11 to 15 years	.55	.004
		From 26 to 30 years > 16 to 20 years	1.66	.021
		More than 30 years > 16 to 20 years	1.63	.035
	Time in the Position	From 26 to 30 years > Less than 6 years	.81	.019
		From 26 to 30 years > From 6 to 10 years	.86	.014
Emotional Control	Age	50 to 59 years > 30 to 39 years	.49	.023
	Time in Company	From 26 to 30 years > 11 to 15 years	.52	.038
		More than 30 years > 11 to 15 years	.74	.030
Inspiring Reading	Working in the training area	Work fully in area > Does not work in area	.65	.0001
		Work fully in area > Part time	.41	.008

education and time within the company, regarding the variance of the "Interaction and Analogy" factor, which compromised the verification of significant differences between the groups' means on this particular factor.

The scores that most differed between groups were related to the factor "Imagination and Introspection," which produced significant differences between nine means. Also in relation to "Emotional Control" and "Inspiring Reading" factor scores, significant differences were found between the means of three and two groups respectively. Among all of the differences found, six were concentrated in subgroups of the variable time within the company, while three other subgroups differed significantly with respect to age. With regard to time within the current job position and working in the same area of training, two subgroups of each point to differences between means. *T* tests were also performed comparing the mean factor scores between men and women. Results show no significant differences ($p < .05$) between these groups although the difference between the mean (.26) for the factor score of "Inspiring Reading" tends to significant ($t\,[683] = 1.683, p = .063$).

Discussion

The results of the statistical validation of the strategies for creating at work measure show clearly that it is a robust factor solution. Besides the satisfactory reliability of its factors, this measure has only two items with factor loadings below .40, another indication of the quality of the solution identified. The evaluation of this measure, however, should not be restricted to these aspects. An important benchmark in the development of the validated instrument was the parallel concept of learning strategies, so that it is arguably possible to compare results obtained with the theoretical structure underlying them. In the content analysis of each first order factor the presence of cognitive, behavioral, and self-regulating strategies was identified, consolidating the relevance of the analogy adopted.

Regarding cognitive strategies, most were concentrated on a single factor, "Flexible Thinking," composed exclusively by these strategies, while other cognitive ones have joined self-regulation strategies in the "Imagination and Introspection" factor, and behavioral strategies on "Interaction and Analogy." Elements such as membership, fluency, analogy, flexibility, and sensitivity to problems are contained in the final factor solution. However, notice must be taken on flexibility and association strategies on one hand (represented by a robust factor), and sensitivity to problems on the other, the latter dispersed in various factors.

The behavioral strategies, unlike the cognitive ones, showed greater cohesion. "Inspiring Reading" adds all items of search for help in written material in the factor solution adopted, in the same way as "Interaction and Analogy," although the latter has seen a greater loss of original items and composed an hybrid factor. In the case of self-regulation strategies, only those related to emotional control are adequately represented, and although some focus and motivation-oriented items have been added to the "Imagination and Introspection" factor, various items constructed for this purpose were not sustained in the final factor solution.

Observing the attributes of the validated measure from the perspective of the creative process, in turn, leads to other interesting considerations. The identification of the steps in the creative process that should benefit the most from the strategies contained in each factor showed the stages of preparation, incubation, and illumination were privileged, while the stages of problem identification and verification were covered less by this factor solution. Although this comparison exercise is inadequate *a priori*, given the limitations of conceptualizing creativity as a linear and systematic process (Bruno-Faria, 2004), its use is seen as a valuable first step in understanding the results of this study, to be further explored as the understanding of strategies for creating at work progresses.

Additional explorations are appropriate in the case of elements whose presence in the final factor solution is weak, such as the aspects regarding sensitivity to problems (refinement and reformulation), and self-regulation of attention and of motivation. It is noteworthy that the absence of certain facets or factors of the latent construct investigated cannot be taken as evidence of its empirical inexistence without further investigation. As suggested by Clark and Watson (1995), it should be considered whether the original items were appropriately worded, if the sample was nonrepresentative of the construct in some important way, or if there were too few items depicting constituent elements of the core construct. Finally, it is necessary also to assess the relevance of the underlying theoretical proposition. That is, the same concerns present in the initial construction of the instrument should be included in efforts of refinement.

Other elements allow some additional considerations about the appropriateness of the developed measure, highlighting the results of discriminant validity and the relationship between strategies for creating and creative self-efficacy at work. As for the moderate correlations found between both these measures, those are theoretically justified by the assumed relationship between self-efficacy and strategies. The first covers the individual's confidence in his or her ability to organize and execute courses of action needed to achieve desired performance (Bandura, 1982; Pajares, 2004). Strategies, in turn, refer to efforts in which individuals effectively engage in order to achieve a certain goal. As both relate to the same type of action (in this case, creative action at work), their relationship is evident, just as observed in learning (Zimmerman, 2000). Despite this affinity, the measures are perfectly distinguished when subjected to joint factor analysis. The preservation of the empirical structure obtained in the discriminant validity analysis, therefore, is another finding pointing to the robustness of the measure proposed here.

The observed relationships between strategies for creating at work and sample characteristics contribute to demonstrate relevance of the proposed construct. As noted in the results, three factors had significant differences ($p < 0.05$) for five sociodemographic variables, indicating that the measure discriminates between groups.

The "Inspiring Reading" factor, for example, showed higher scores among those who work entirely within their area of formal training, as opposed to those who do not work or work only partially in their area of training. A likely explanation is that formal education in the same work area enables professionals to seek help at adequate sources, while those without such training do not have the same access or do not use the reading material with the same ease.

Older professionals who have spent more time in the company, in turn, had higher factor scores on "Emotional Control." It is assumed that this effect may result, in part, from individuals' maturity, which would favor the use of self-regulation strategies. The time with the company, on the other hand, would act in the sense that veterans in the organization would feel more comfortable to use some strategies that involve temporary cessation of activities, such as those present in this factor.

In the "Imagination and Introspection" factor, a similar effect seems to occur, given that older professionals, with more time in the company and more time spent in their current role had higher scores on this factor. That is, the originality built into some of these strategies would be more accessible to those who had more familiarity with their tasks, the organization, and themselves. The exception would be for job position, as managers showed lower scores compared to those who are employed in administrative support. As the exercise of managerial function often requires alignment with the status quo, managers are expected to have lower scores on this factor grouping strategies that focus on what is different and unusual.

As to the "Flexible Thinking" factor, there were no significant differences between groups' means. In this case, one must question whether the present sample had sufficient variation in relation to this factor. The same was true for "Interaction and Analogy"; however, given the violation of a requirement for completion of the ANOVAs, there are no grounds for assuming a lack of significant difference. In any case, it seems appropriate to understand this occurrence as a possible point to be improved in subsequent versions of the measure of Strategies for Creating at Work, ensuring for these factors the adequate presence of items that discriminate between the respondents regarding the use of such strategies (Clark & Watson, 1995).

Because of its uniqueness, the results observed in Strategies for Creating at Work do not allow comparison with previous studies. However, these results are interpretable and consistent with other studies of learning strategies at work, where there are significant relationships between individual variables and the use of these strategies (e.g., Lopes-Ribeiro, 2005; Pantoja, 2004).

The decisions made in the development of this measure were aimed at obtaining a robust and parsimonious factor solution. Thus, the researchers did not refrain from promoting the exclusion of items required for this purpose. In fact, the results indicate that this goal was reached, whereas the developed measure of Strategies for Creating at Work demonstrates psychometric qualities and satisfying theoretical attributes. Nevertheless, suggestions and recommendations for its improvement herein should be considered in future efforts to refine the measure, taking into account the complexity of the work required for proposing an original and reliable instrument to measure the concept in focus.

Conclusion

The results point not only to the existence of the concept of strategies for creating at work, but also to the adequacy of the developed measure and the path used in the formulation of both. It is expected that this measure will contribute to the development of more complex research designs, which consider the individual-context interaction and deepen the knowledge available about them, perhaps offering elements to promote a better individual-work fit and optimizing the use of creative potential. This work, therefore, intends to be a precursor to such studies.

Finally, it is worth commenting on its usefulness in organizations, because it may constitute an important diagnostic tool, providing support to managers who wish to encourage the creative potential of employees. Also noteworthy is the possibility of establishing contextual factors associated with the use of certain strategies, or identifying strategies to be encouraged and developed. Therefore, the concept of strategies for creating at work can greatly contribute to the advancement of studies on creativity in organizations, as well as to individual creative performance in these organizations.

REFERENCES

Abbad, G., & Borges-Andrade, J. E. (2004). Aprendizagem humana em organizações e trabalho [Human learning in organizations and work]. In J. C. Zanelli, J. E. Borges-Andrade, & A. V. B. Bastos (Eds.), *Psicologia, organizações e trabalho no Brasil* [Psychology, organizations and work in Brazil] (pp. 237–275). Porto Alegre, Brazil: Artmed.

Adams, J. L. (1986). Conceptual blockbusting. A pleasurable guide to better problem solving. New York, NY: Norton.

Alamshah, E. (1972). Blockages to creativity. *The Journal of Creative Behavior, 6,* 105–113.

Alencar, E. M. L. S. (1974a). *A study of creativity training in elementary grades in Brazilian schools* (Unpublished doctoral dissertation). Purdue University, West Lafayette, IN.

Alencar, E. M. L. S. (1974b). Avaliação da criatividade de alunos por professores [Students' creative abilities assessment by teachers]. *Interamerican Journal of Psychology, 8,* 219–224.

Alencar, E. M. L. S. (1994). Creativity in the Brazilian educational context: Two decades of research. *Gifted and Talented International, 9,* 4–7.

Alencar, E. M. L. S. (1995a). Challenges to the development of the creative talent. *Gifted and Talented International, 10,* 5–8.

Alencar, E. M. L. S. (1995b). *Criatividade [Creativity].* Brasilia, Brazil: Editora da Universidade de Brasilia.

Alencar, E. M. L. S. (1995c). Developing creativity at the university level. *European Journal for High Ability, 6,* 82–90.

Alencar, E. M. L. S. (1996). University students' evaluation of their own level of creativity and their teachers' and colleagues' level of creativity. *Gifted Education International, 11,* 128–130.

Alencar, E. M. L. S. (1997a). *A gerência da criatividade* [Managing creativity]. São Paulo, Brazil: Makron Books.

Alencar, E. M. L. S. (1997b). O estímulo à criatividade no contexto universitário [Fostering creativity in the university context]. *Psicologia Escolar e Educacional, 1,* 29–37.

Alencar, E. M. L. S. (1998). Personality traits of Brazilian creative scientists. *Gifted and Talented International, 13,* 14–18.

Alencar, E. M. L. S. (1999). Barreiras à criatividade pessoal: Desenvolvimento de um instrumento de medida [Obstacles to personal creativity: Development of a measurement instrument]. *Psicologia Escolar e Educacional, 3,* 123–132.

Alencar, E. M. L. S. (2000a). *Como desenvolver o potencial criador* [How to develop the creative potential] (8th ed.). Petrópolis, Brazil: Vozes.

Alencar, E. M. L. S. (2000b). O perfil do professor facilitador e do professor inibidor da criatividade segundo estudantes de pós-graduação [Characteristics of the creativity facilitating and the creativity inhibiting profesor according to graduate students]. *Boletim da Academia Paulista de Psicologia, 19,* 84–94.

Alencar, E. M. L. S. (2000c). *O processo de criatividade* [The creative process]. São Paulo, Brazil: MAKRON Books.

Alencar, E. M. L. S. (2001a). *Criatividade e educação do superdotado [Creativity and the education of the gifted].* Petrópolis, Brazil: Vozes.

Alencar, E. M. L. S. (2001b). Obstacles to personal creativity among university students. *Gifted Education International, 15,* 133–140.

Alencar, E. M. L. S. (2002a). *Mastering creativity for education in the 21th century.* Proceedings of the Biennial World Conference of the World Council for Gifted and Talented Children (pp. 13–21). Northridge, CA: World Council for Gifted and Talented Children.

Alencar, E. M. L. S. (2002b). O contexto educacional e sua influência na criatividade [The educational context and its influence on creativity]. *Linhas Críticas, 8,* 165–178.

Alencar, E. M. L. S. (2002c). O estímulo à criatividade em programas de pós-graduação segundo seus estudantes [The incentive to creativity in graduate programs according to the students]. *Psicologia: Reflexão e Crítica, 15,* 63–69.

Alencar, E. M. L. S. (2005). *A gerência da criatividade* [Managing creativity]. São Paulo, Brazil: Makron.

Alencar, E. M. L. S. (2007). O papel da escola na estimulação do talento criativo [The role of school in the incentive of the creative talent]. In D. S. Fleith & E. M. L. S. Alencar (Eds.), *Desenvolvimento de talentos e altas habilidades. Orientação a pais e professores* [Talent and high ability development. Guidelines for parents and teachers] (pp. 151–162). Porto Alegre, Brazil: ArtMed.

Alencar, E. M. L. S., Collares, K., Dias, L., & Julião, S. (1993, October). *Efeitos a curto e médio prazos de um programa de treinamento de criatividade em estudantes do ensino de segundo grau* [Short and medium term effects of a creativity training program in secondary school students]. Paper presented at the XXIII Anual Meeting of the Brazilian Society of Psychology, Ribeirão Preto, Brazil.

Alencar, E. M. L. S., & Fleith, D. S. (2003a). Barreiras à criatividade pessoal entre professores de distintos níveis de ensino [Obstacles to personal creativity among teachers from diferent educational levels]. *Psicologia: Reflexão e Crítica, 16,* 63–69.

Alencar, E. M. L. S., & Fleith, D. S. (2003b). *Criatividade. Múltiplas perspectivas* [Creativity: Multiple perspectives]. Brasilia, Brazil: Editora da UnB.

Alencar E. M. L. S., & Fleith, D. S. (2003c). Contribuições teóricas recentes ao estudo da criatividade [Recent theoretical contributions to the study of creativity]. *Psicologia: Teoria e Pesquisa, 19,* 1–8.

Alencar, E. M. L. S., & Fleith, D. S. (2004a). *Barreiras à criatividade pessoal e sua relação com fatores individuais e sociais* [Obstacles to personal creativity and its relationship with individual and social factors]. Report No. 47419/01-8). Brasilia, Brazil: Brazilian Council for the Scientific and Technological Development.

Alencar, E. M. L. S., & Fleith, D. S. (2004b). Creativity in university courses: Perceptions of professors and students. *Gifted and Talented International, 19,* 24–28.

Alencar, E. M. L. S., & Fleith, D. S. (2007). Escala de práticas pedagógicas para a criatividade no ensino fundamental: estudo preliminar de validação [Scale of pedagogical practices for creativity in the elementary school level: A preliminary study of validation]. *Psicologia em Interação, 11,* 231–239.

Alencar, E. M. L. S., Fleith, D. S., Gramkow, G., Ribeiro, R. A., Silva, F. L., Vasconcelos, L. C., . . . & Kohlsdorf, M. (2003, October). *Um estudo de validade concorrente do Inventário de Barreiras à Criatividade Pessoal* [A study of concurrent validity of the Obstacles to Personal Creativity Inventory]. Paper presented at the XXXV Annual Meeting of the Brazilian Society of Psychology, Belo Horizonte, Brazil.

Alencar, E. M. L. S., Fleith, D. S., & Martínez, A. M. (2003). Obstacles to creativity among Brazilian and Mexican university students: A comparative study. *The Journal of Creative Behavior, 37,* 179–192.

Alencar, E. M. L. S., Fleith, D. S., & Virgolim, A. M. R. (1995). Fatores inibidores à criatividade em estudantes universitários e professores [Inhibiting factors to creativity in university students and teachers]. In R. S. L. Guzzo, G. P. Witter, S. Pfromm Netto, E. Rosado, & S. Wechsler (Eds.), *O futuro da criança na escola, família e sociedade* [The future of the child in school, family and society] (pp. 105–109). Campinas, Brazil: Editora Átomo.

Alencar, E. M. L. S., & Martínez, A. M. (1998). Barreiras à expressão da criatividade entre profissionais brasileiros, cubanos e portugueses [Barriers to the expression of creativity among Brazilian, Cuban and Portuguese professionals]. *Psicologia Escolar e Educacional, 2,* 23–32.

Alencar, E. M. L. S., Oliveira, A. C., Ribeiro, R., & Brandão, S. N. (1996, October). *Barreiras à expressão da criatividade entre profissionais da área de educação* [Barriers to the expression of creativity among professionals in education]. Paper presented at the XXVI Annual Meeting of the Brazilian Society of Psychology, Ribeirão Preto, Brazil.

Amabile, T. M. (1983). *The social psychology of creativity*. New York, NY: Springer-Verlag.

Amabile, T. M. (1989). *Growing up creative*. Buffalo, NY: The Creative Education Foundation Press.

Amabile, T. M. (1995). Discovering the unknowable, managing the unmanageable. In C. M. Ford & D. A. Gioia (Eds.), *Creative action in organizations. Ivory tower visions & real world voices* (pp. 77–82). London, England: Sage.

Amabile, T. M. (1996a, January). Creativity and innovation in organizations. *Harvard Business School*, 1–15.

Amabile, T. M. (1996b). *Creativity in context*. Boulder, CO: Westview Press.

Amabile, T. M. (1997). Motivating creativity in organizations: On doing what you love and loving what you do. *California Management Review, 40,* 39–58.

Amabile, T. M. (1999, January/February). Como não matar a criatividade [How not to kill creativity]. *HSM Management,* 110–116.

Amabile, T. M., & Gryskiewicz, N. D. (1989). The creative environment scales: Work Environment Inventory. *Creativity Research Journal, 2,* 231–253.

Ambrose, M. L., & Kulik, C. T. (1999). Old friends, new faces: Motivation research in the 1990s. *Journal of Management, 5,* 231–292.

Anastasi, A. (1988). *Psychological testing.* New York, NY: MacMillan.

Arieti, S. (1976). *Creativity. The magic synthesis.* New York, NY: Basic Books.

Balka, D. S. (1974). Creative ability in mathematics. *Arithmetic Teacher, 21,* 633–636.

Bandura, A. (1982). Self-efficacy mechanism in human agency. *American Psychologist, 37,* 122–147.

Borges-Andrade, J. E., Coelho, Jr., F. A., & Queiroga, F. (2006). *Pesquisa sobre micro comportamento organizacional no Brasil: "O estado da arte"* [Research on micro organizational behavior in Brazil: "The state of the art"]. Paper presented at the Second Brazilian Congress on Work and Organizational Psychology, Brasilia, Brazil.

Brazil. (1997). *Parâmetros curriculares nacionais: Matemática (1a a 4a séries)* [National curricular guidelines: Mathematics (1st–4th grades)]. Brasilia, Brazil: MEC/ SEF.

Brazil. (1998). *Parâmetros curriculares nacionais: Matemática (5a a 8a séries)* [National curricular guidelines: Mathematics (5th–8th grades)]. Brasilia, Brazil: MEC/ SEF.

Brazil. (1999). *Parâmetros curriculares nacionais: Ensino médio. Ciências da natureza, matemática e suas tecnologias* [National curricular guidelines: Secondary school. Nature sciences, mathematics and technologies]. Brasilia, Brazil: MEC/SEMT.

Bruno-Faria, M. F. (1996). *Estímulos e barreiras à criatividade no ambiente de trabalho de uma instituição bancária* [Incentives and obstacles to creativity in the work place in a bank corporation] (Unpublished master's thesis). University of Brasilia, Brazil.

Bruno-Faria, M. F. (2003). Criatividade, inovação e mudança organizacional [Creativity, innovation and organizational change]. In S. M. V. Lima (Ed.), *Mudança organizacional: Teoria e gestão* [Organizational change: Theory and management] (pp. 111–141). Rio de Janeiro, Brazil: FGV.

Bruno-Faria, M. F. (2004). *O processo criativo em indivíduos e grupos participantes de projetos inovadores* [The creative process in individuals and groups participating in innovative projects] (Unpublished doctoral dissertation). University of Brasilia, Brazil.

Bruno-Faria, M. F. (2005). Contribuições da teoria da subjetividade e da epistemologia qualitativa para a compreensão do processo criativo no contexto organizacional [Contributions of the theory of subjectivity and qualitative epistemology to the understanding of the creative process in the organizational context]. In F. G. Rey (Ed.), *Subjetividade, complexidade e pesquisa em psicologia* [Subjectivity, complexity and research in psychology] (pp. 155–190). São Paulo, Brazil: Pioneira Thomson Learning.

Bruno-Faria, M. F., & Alencar, E. M. L. S. (1996). Estímulos e barreiras à criatividade no ambiente de trabalho [Stimulants and barriers to creativity in the workplace]. *Revista de Administração, 31,* 50–61.

Bruno-Faria, M. F., & Alencar, E. M. L. S. (1998). Indicadores de clima para a criatividade: Um instrumento de medida da percepção de estímulos e barreiras à criatividade no ambiente de trabalho [Indicators of climate for creativity: A measurement instrument of incentives and obstacles to creativity in the work environment]. *Revista de Administração, 33,* 86–91.

Bruno-Faria, M. F., Veiga, H., & Macêdo, L. (2008). Criatividade nas organizações: análise da produção científica nacional em periódicos e livros de Administração e Psicologia [Creativity in organizations: Brazilian scientific production in Administration and Psychology journals and books]. *Revista Psicologia: Organizações e Trabalho, 8,* 142–163.

Burnside, R. M. (1995). The soft stuff is the hard stuff: Encouraging creativity in times of turbulence. *Compensation & Benefits Management, 11*(3), 58–64.

Burnside, R. M., Amabile, T. M., & Gryskiewicz, N. D. (1988). Assessing organizational climates for creativity and innovation-methodological review of large company audits. In Y. Ijiri & R. L. Kuhn (Eds.), *New directions in creative and innovative management. Bringing theory and practice* (pp. 169–185). Cambridge: Ballinger.

Callahan, C. M. (1991). The assessment of creativity. In N. Colangelo & G. A. Davis (Eds.), *Handbook of gifted education* (pp. 219–235). Needham Heights, MA: Allyn and Bacon.

Castanho, M. E. L. M. (2000). A criatividade na sala de aula universitária [Creativity in university classes]. In I. P. Veiga & M. E. L. M. Castanho (Eds.), *Pedagogia universitária. A aula em foco* [University pedagogy. Focus on the classroom] (pp. 75–89). São Paulo, Brazil: Papirus.

Castro, J. S. R. (2007). *Criatividade escolar: relação entre tempo de experiência docente e tipo de escola* [Creativity in schools: Relationship between teaching experience and school type] (Unpublished master's thesis). University of Brasilia, Brazil.

Choi, J. N. (2004). Individual and contextual predictors of creative performance: The mediating role of psychological processes. *Creativity Research Journal, 16,* 187–199.

Clark, L. A., & Watson, D. (1995). Constructing validity: Basic issues in objective scale development. *Psychological Assessment, 7,* 309–319.

Cohen, D. (1997, September). Singapore wants its universities to encourage more creativity. *The Chronicle of Higher Education,* 71–72.

Cole, D. G., Sugioka, H. L., & Yamagata-Lynch, L. C. (1999). Supportive classroom environments for creativity in higher education. *Journal of Creative Behavior, 33,* 277–292.

Costello, A. B., & Osborne, J. W. (2005). Best practices in exploratory factor analysis: Four recommendations for getting the most from your analysis. *Practical Assessment Research & Evaluation, 10.* Retrieved from http://pareonline.net/getvn.asp?v=10&n=7

Craft, A. (1998). Educator perspectives on creativity: An English study. *Journal of Creative Behavior, 32,* 244–256.

Craft, A. (2005). *Creativity in schools. Tensions and dilemmas.* London, England: Routledge.

Craft, A. (2006). Creativity in schools. In N. Jackson, M. Oliver, M. Shaw, & J. Wisdom (Eds.), *Developing creativity in higher education* (pp. 19–28). London, England: Routledge.

Cramond, B. (1999). Going beyond the scores of the Torrance Tests of Creative Thinking. In A. S. Fishkin, B. Cramond, & P. Olszewski-Kubilius (Eds.), *Investigating creativity in youth* (pp. 307–327). Creskill, NJ: Hampton Press.

Cramond, B., Matthews-Morgan, J., Bandalos, D., & Zuo, L. (2005). A report on the 40-year follow-up of the Torrance Tests of Creative Thinking: Alive and well in the new millennium. *Gifted Child Quarterly, 49,* 283–291.

Crespo, M. L. F. (2004). Construção de uma medida de clima criativo em organizações [Development of a creative climate in organizations measurement]. *Estudos de Psicologia PUCCAMP, 21,* 91–99.

Crockenberg, S. B. (1972). Creativity tests: A boon or boondoggle for education? *Review of Educational Research, 42,* 17–45.

Cropley, A. J. (1997). Fostering creativity in the classroom: General principles. In M. A. Runco (Ed.), *The creativity research book* (pp. 83–114). Cresskill, NJ: Hampton Press.

Cropley, A. J. (2005). *Creativity in education and learning: A guide for teachers and educators.* London, England: Routledge.

Cropley, A. J. (2006). Creativity: A social approach. *Roeper Review, 28,* 125–130.

Cropley, A. J., & Urban, K. K. (2000). Programs and strategies for nurturing creativity. In K. A. Heller, F. J. Mönks, R. J. Sternberg, & R. F. Subotnik

(Eds.), *International handbook of giftedness and talent* (pp. 485–498). Oxford, England: Elsevier Science.

Csikszentmihalyi, M. (1988). Society, culture, and person: A systems view of creativity. In R. J. Sternberg (Ed.), *The nature of creativity* (pp. 325–339). New York, NY: Cambridge University Press.

Csikszentmihalyi, M. (1994). The domain of creativity. In D. H. Feldman, M. Csikszentmihalyi, & H. Gardner (Eds.), *Changing the world. A framework for the study of creativity* (pp. 135–158). Westport, CT: Praeger.

Csikszentmihalyi, M. (1996). *Creativity: Flow and the psychology of discovery and invention.* New York, NY: HarperCollins.

Csikszentmihalyi, M. (1999). Implications of a systems perspective for the study of creativity. In R. J. Sternberg (Ed.), *Handbook of creativity* (pp. 313–335). New York, NY: Cambridge University Press.

Csikszentmihalyi, M. (2006). Developing creativity. In N. Jackson, M. Oliver, M. Shaw, & J. Wisdom (Eds.), *Developing creativity in higher education* (pp. xviii–xx). London, England: Routledge.

Csikszentmihalyi, M., & Sawyer, K. (1995). Creative insight: The social dimension of a solitary moment. In R. J. Sternberg & J. E. Davidson (Eds.), *The nature of insight* (pp. 329–364). Cambridge, MA: The MIT Press.

D'Ambrósio, U. (2004). Um enfoque transdisciplinar à educação e à história da matemática [A transdisciplinary focus on education and mathematics]. In M. A. V. Bicudo & M. C. Borba (Eds.), *Educação matemática: pesquisa em movimento* [Mathematics education: Research in movement] (pp. 13–29). São Paulo, Brazil: Cortez.

Davis, G. A., & Rimm, S. G. (1982). Groups Inventory for Finding Interests (GIFFI I and II): Instruments for identifying creative potential in the junior and senior high school. *Journal of Creative Behavior, 16,* 50–57.

Dante, L. R. (1980). *Incentivando a criatividade através da educação matemática* [Fostering creativity through mathematics education] (Unpublished doctoral dissertation). Catholic University of São Paulo, Brazil.

Dante, L. R. (1988). *Criatividade e resolução de problemas na prática educativa matemática* [Creativity and problem solving in the educational practice in mathematics] (Thesis of free teaching). Paulista State University, Rio Claro, São Paulo, Brazil.

Dunn, J. A. (1975). Tests of creativity in mathematics. *International Journal of Mathematical Education in Science and Technology, 6,* 327–332.

Eccles, J. S., & Wigfield, A. (2002). Motivational beliefs, values and goals. *Annual Review of Psychology, 53,* 109–32.

Fagerberg, J. (2006). Innovation: A guide to the literature. In J. Fagerberg, D. C. Mowery, & R. R. Nelson. (Eds.), *The Oxford handbook of innovation* (pp. 1–26). New York, NY: Oxford University.

Finaciadora de Estudos e Projetos. (2004). *Lei de incentivo à inovação [Incentive to innovation law]*. Retrieved from http://www.finep.gov.br/imprensa/sala_imprensa/lei_de_inovacao_redacao_final.pdf

Fleith, D. S. (2000). Teacher and student perceptions of creativity in the classroom environment. *Roeper Review, 22,* 148–153.

Fleith, D. S. (2001). Criatividade: novos conceitos e ideias. Aplicabilidade à educação [Creativity: New concepts and ideas. Application to education]. *Cadernos de Educação Especial, 17,* 55–61.

Fleith, D. S. (2002). Ambientes educacionais que promovem a criatividade e excelência [Educational environments that promote creativity and excellence]. *Sobredotação, 3,* 27–39.

Fleith, D. S. (2011). Creativity in the Brazilian culture. *Online Readings in Psychology and Culture*, Unit 4. Retrieved from http://scholarworks.gvsu.edu/orpc/vol4/iss3/3

Fleith, D. S., & Alencar, E. M. L. S. (1992). Medidas de criatividade [Creativity measures]. *Psicologia: Teoria e Pesquisa, 8,* 319–326.

Fleith, D. S., & Alencar, E. M. L. S. (2005). Escala sobre o clima para criatividade em sala de aula [Scale of the classroom climate for creativity]. *Psicologia: Teoria e Pesquisa, 21,* 85–91.

Fleith, D. S., & Alencar, E. M. L. S. (2006). Percepção de alunos do ensino fundamental quanto ao clima de sala de aula para criatividade [Elementary grade students' perception with respect to the classroom climate for creativity]. *Psicologia em Estudo, 11,* 513–521.

Fleith, D. S., & Alencar, E. M. L. S. (2008). Características personológicas e fatores ambientais relacionados à criatividade do aluno do ensino fundamental [Individual characteristics and environmental factors associated with elementary grade student]. *Avaliação Psicológica, 7,* 35–44.

Fleith, D. S., Rodrigues, M. A. M., Viana, M. C. A., & Cerqueira, T. C. S. (2000). The creation process of Brazilian musicians. *The Journal of Creative Behavior, 34,* 61–75.

Floyd, F. J., & Widaman, K. F. (1995). Factor analysis in the development and refinement of clinical assessment instruments. *Psychological Assessment, 16,* 187–199.

Fonseca, C. A. M. (2001). *Criatividade e comprometimento organizacional: suas relações com a percepção de desempenho no trabalho* [Creativity and organizational commitment: Its relationships with the perception of work performance] (Unpublished master's thesis). Federal Univeristy of Bahia, Salvador, Brazil.

Foster, J. (1970). An exploratory attempt to assess creative ability in mathematics. *Primary Teacher, 8,* 2–8.

Furman, A. (1998). Teacher and pupil characteristics in the perception of the creativity of classroom climate. *The Journal of Creative Behavior, 32,* 258–277.

Gable, R. K., & Wolf, M. B. (1993). *Instrument development in the affective domain* (2nd ed.). Norwell, MA: Kluwer Academic.

Gall, M. D., Borg, W. R., & Gall, J. P. (1996). *Educational research* (6th ed.). White Plains, NY: Longman.

Getzels, J. W., & Csikszentmihalyi, M. (1975). From problem solving to problem finding. In I. A. Taylor & J. W. Getzels (Eds.), *Perspectives in creativity* (pp. 90–116). Chicago, IL: Aldine.

Gimenez, F. (1993). Estratégia de criatividade em pequenas empresas [Creative strategies in small businesses]. *Revista de Administração, 28,* 72–82.

Gontijo, C. H. (2006, July). *Resolução e formulação de problemas: Caminhos para o desenvolvimento da criatividade em matemática* [Problem solving and identification: Ways to the development of creativity in mathematics]. Paper presented at the I International Simposium of Mathematics Education, Recife, Pernambuco, Brazil.

Gontijo, C. H. (2007). *Relação entre criatividade, criatividade em matemática e motivação em matemática de alunos do ensino médio* [Creativity, creativity in mathematics, and motivation towards mathematics of secondary school students] (Unpublished doctoral dissertation). Universty of Brasilia, Brazil.

Greeno, J. G. (1989). A perspective in thinking. *American Psychologist, 44,* 134–141.

Guilford, J. P. (1950). Creativity. *American Psychologist, 5,* 444–454.

Guilford, J. P. (1967). *The nature of human intelligence.* New York, NY: McGraw-Hill.

Günther, H. (1996). Desenvolvimento de instrumento para levantamento de dados (*survey*) [Development of an instrument to collect data (survey)]. In L. Pasquali (Ed.), *Teoria e métodos de medida em ciências do comportamento* [Theory and measurement methods of the behavioral sciences] (pp. 387–418). Brasilia, Brazil: UnB-INEP.

Hashimoto, Y. (1997). The methods of fostering creativity through mathematical problem solving. *International Reviews on Mathematical Education, 29,* 8–87.

Haylock, D. W. (1985). Conflicts in the assessment and encouragement of mathematical creativity in schoolchildren. *International Journal of Mathematical Education in Science and Technology, 16,* 547–553.

Haylock, D. W. (1987). A framework for assessing mathematical creativity in schoolchildren. *Educational Studies in Mathematics, 18,* 59–74.

Haylock, D. W. (1997). Recognizing mathematical creativity in schoolchildren. *The International Reviews on Mathematical Education, 29,* 68–74.

Hill, K. G., & Amabile, T. (1993). A social psychological perspective on creativity: Intrinsic motivation and creativity in the classroom and workplace. In S. G. Isaksen, M. G. Murdock, R. L. Firestein, & D. J. Treffinger (Eds.), *Understanding and recognizing creativity: The emergence of a discipline* (pp. 400–432). Norwood, NJ: Abex.

Hocevar, D., & Bachelor, P. (1989). A taxonomy and critique of measurements used in the study of creativity. In J. A. Glover, R. R. Ronning, & C. R. Reynolds (Eds.), *Handbook of creativity* (pp. 53–76). New York, NY: Plenum Press.

Holman, D., Epitropaki, O., & Fernie, S. (2001). Understanding learning strategies in the workplace: A factor analytic investigation. *Journal of Occupational and Organizational Psychology, 74,* 675–681.

Johnson, A. S., & Fishkin, A. S. (1999). Assessment of cognitive and affective behaviors related to creativity. In A. S. Fishkin, B. Cramond, & P. Olszewski-Kubilius (Eds.), *Investigating creativity in youth* (pp. 265–306). Creskill, NJ: Hampton Press.

Joly, M. C. R., & Guerra, P. B. C. (2004). Compreensão em leitura e barreiras à criatividade: Um estudo com universitários ingressantes [Reading comprehension and barriers to creativity: A study with college freshment]. *Psico, 35,* 151–159.

Jones, L. (1993). Barriers to creativity and their relationship to individual, group, and organizational behavior. In S. G. Isaksen, M. C. Mordock, R. L. Firestien, & D. J. Treffinger (Eds.), *Nurturing and developing creativity: The emergence of a discipline* (pp. 133–154). Norwood, NJ: Ablex.

Kerr, B. (2000). Guiding gifted girls and young women. In K. A. Heller, J. F. Mönks, R. J. Sternberg, & R. F. Subotnik (Eds.), *International handbook of research and development of giftedness and talent* (2nd ed., pp. 649–657). Oxford, England: Elsevier Science.

Khatena, J., & Torrance, E. P. (1976). *Khatena-Torrance Creative Perception Inventory. Something about myself.* Bensenville, IL: Scholastic Testing Service.

Kirton, M. J. (1987). Adaptors and innovators: Cognitive style and personality. In S. G. Isaksen (Ed.), *Frontiers of creativity research: Beyond the basics* (pp. 282–304). Buffalo, NY: Bearly.

Krutetskii, V. A. (1976). *The psychology of mathematical abilities in schoolchildren.* Chicago, IL: The University of Chicago Press.

Laros, J. A. (2004). O uso da análise fatorial: algumas diretrizes para pesquisadores [The use of factor analysis: Some guidelines for researchers]. In L. Pasquali. (Ed.), *Análise fatorial para pesquisadores* [Factor analysis for researchers] (pp. 147–170). Petrópolis, Brazil: Vozes.

Latham, G. P., & Pinder, C. P. (2005). Work motivation theory and research at the dawn of the twenty-first century. *Annual Review of Psychology, 56,* 485–516.

Lee, K. S., Hwang, D., & Seo, J. J. (2003). A development of the test for mathematical creative problem solving ability. *Journal of The Korea Society of Mathematical Education, 7,* 163–189.

Lima, S. M. V. (2003). *Estudo longitudinal das relações entre gestão e inovação tecnológica* [Longitudinal study of relations between management and technological innovation]. Unpublished manuscript, EMBRAPA, Brasilia, Brazil.

Livne, N. L., Livne, O. E., & Milgram, R. M. (1999). Assessing academic and creative abilities in mathematics at four levels of understanding. *International Journal of Mathematical Education in Science & Technology, 30,* 227–243.

Livne, N. L., & Milgram, R. M. (2000). Assessing four levels of creative mathematical ability in Israeli adolescents utilizing out-of-school activities: A circular three-stage technique. *Roeper Review, 22,* 111–116.

Livne, N. L., & Milgram, R. M. (2006). Academic versus creative abilities in mathematics: Two components of the same construct? *Creativity Research Journal, 18,* 199–212.

Lopes-Ribeiro, R. (2005). *Motivação para aprendizagem informal no trabalho: construção de medidas e investigação de modelo teórico* [Motivation for informal learning at work: Measure development and investigation of theoretical model] (Unpublished master's thesis). University of Brasilia, Brazil.

Lubart, T. (1999). Creativity across culture. In R. J. Sternberg (Ed.), Handbook of creativity (pp. 339–350). New York, NY: Cambridge University Press.

Lubart, T. (2007). *Psicologia da criatividade* [Psychology of creativity]. Porto Alegre, Brazil: ArtMed.

Lubart, T., & Guignard, H. H. (2004). The generality-specificity of creativity: A multivariate approach. In R. J. Sternberg, E. L. Grigorenko, & J. L. Singer

(Eds.), *Creativity. From potential to realization* (pp. 43–56). Washington, DC: American Psychological Association.

MacKinnon, D. W. (1978). *In search of human effectiveness: Identifying and developing creativity*. Buffalo, NY: The Creative Education Foundation.

MacKinnon, D. W. (1982). The personality correlates of creativity: Study of American architects. In P. E. Vernon (Ed.), *Creativity* (pp. 289–311). Harmondsworth, England: Penguin.

Martínez, A. M. (2006). Criatividade no trabalho pedagógico e criatividade na aprendizagem: Uma relação necessária? [Creativity in the pedagogy and creativity in the learning process: Is it a possible relationship?] In M. C. Tacca (Ed.), *Aprendizagem e trabalho pedagógico* [Learning and pedagogical work] (pp. 69–94). Campinas, Brazil: Alínea.

Maslow, A. H. (1959). Creativity in self-actualizing people. In H. H. Anderson (Ed.), *Creativity and its cultivation* (pp. 83–95). New York, NY: Harper & Row.

Mathisen, G. E., & Einarsen, S. (2004). A review of instruments assessing creative and innovative environments within organizations. *Creativity Research Journal, 16*, 119–140.

Matos, D. R., & Fleith, D. S. (2006). Criatividade e clima criativo entre alunos de escolas abertas, intermediárias e tradicionais [Creativity and creative climate among students from open, intermediary, and traditional school]. *Psicologia Escolar e Educacional, 10,* 109–120.

Michael, W. B. (2003). Guilford's Structure of Intellect and structure-of-intellect problem-solving models. In J. Houtz (Ed.), *The educational psychology of creativity* (pp. 167–198). Cresskill, NJ: Hampton Press.

Michael, W. B., & Wright, C. R. (1989). Psychometric issues in the assessment of creativity. In J. A. Glover, R. R. Ronning, & C. R. Reynolds (Eds.), *Handbook of creativity* (pp. 32–52). New York, NY: Plenum.

Moore, D. S. (2000). *The basic practice of statistics*. New York, NY: Freeman.

Montuori, A., & Purser, R. E. (1995). Deconstructing the lone genius myth: Toward a contextual view of creativity. *Journal of Humanistic Psychology, 35,* 69–112.

Moraes, M. M. (2006). *Auto-eficácia e estratégias para criar no trabalho: Construção de medidas* [Self-efficacy and creative strategies at work: Measure development] (Unpublished master's thesis). University of Brasilia, Brasilia, Brazil.

Moraes, M. M., & Lima, S. M. V. (2008). *Creative strategies at work: Theoretical proposition and measure development.* Paper presented at the Conference on Work, Well-being and Performance: New Perspectives for the Modern Workplace, Sheffield, UK.

Moreira, D. A., & Queiroz, A. C. (2007). Inovação: conceitos fundamentais [Innovation: Fundamental concepts]. In D. A. Moreira & A. C.Queiroz (Eds.), *Inovação organizacional e tecnológica* [Organizational and technological innovation] (pp. 1–22). São Paulo, Brazil: Thomson Learning.

Muir, A. (1988). The psychology of mathematical creativity. *The Mathematical Intelligencer, 10,* 33–37.

Nakamura, J., & Csikszentmihalyi, M. (2003). Creativity in later life. In R. K. Sawyer (Ed.), *Creativity and development* (pp. 186–216). New York, NY: Oxford University Press.

Nakano, T. C., & Wechsler, S. M. (2007). Identificação e avaliação do talento criativo [The identification and assessment of creative talent]. In D. S. Fleith & E. M. L. S. Alencar (Eds.), *Desenvolvimento de talentos e altas habilidades. Orientação a pais e professores* [Talent and high ability development. Guidelines for parents and teachers] (pp. 87–98). Porto Alegre, Brazil: ArtMed.

Necka, E. (1992). *Creativity training.* Cracov, Poland: Universitas.

Necka, E. (1994, October). *Teaching creativity in the classroom. General principles and some practical methods.* Paper presented at the International Conference of Education for the Future, São Paulo, Brazil.

Novaes, M. H. (1992). *Psicologia da educação e prática profissional* [Educational psychology and professional practice]. Petrópolis, Brazil: Vozes.

Novaes, M. H. (1999). *Compromisso ou alienação frente ao próximo século* [Commitment or alienation toward the next century]. Rio de Janeiro, Brazil: Nau.

Oliver, M., Shah, B., McGoldrick, C., & Edwards, M. (2006). Students' experiences of creativity. In N. Jackson, M. Oliver, M. Shaw, & J. Wisdom (Eds.), *Developing creativity in higher education* (pp. 43–58). London, England: Routledge.

Pajares, F. (2004). *Overview of social cognitive theory and of self-efficacy.* Retrieved from http://www.emory.edu/EDUCATION/mfp/eff.html

Pantoja, M. J. (2004). *Estratégias de aprendizagem no trabalho e percepções de suporte à aprendizagem—uma análise multinível* [Learning strategies in the workplace and perceptions of learning support—a multilevel analysis] (Unpublished doctoral dissertation). University of Brasilia, Brazil.

Parnes, S. J. (1967). *Creative behavior guidebook.* New York, NY: Scribner's.

Parolin, S. R. H., Bosquetti, M. A., Chang, Jr., Albuquerque, L. G., & Santos, N. L. (2007, September). *Etapa de processo de validação de instrumento de percepção da criatividade no ambiente organizacional pela ótica dos empregados* [Validation process of an instrument to measure creativity in the organizational enviroment according to employees]. Paper presented at the XXXI ANPAD Meeting, Rio de Janeiro, Brazil.

Pasquali, L. (1997). *Psicometria: teoria e aplicações* [Psychometry: Theory and applications]. Brasilia, Brazil: Editora da UnB.

Pasquali, L. (2001). Parâmetros psicométricos dos testes psicológicos [Psychometric parameters of psychological tests]. In L. Pasquali (Ed.), *Fundamentos das técnicas psicológicas* [Psychological techniques basis] (pp. 111–136). São Paulo, Brazil: Casa do Psicólogo.

Paulovich, A. (1993). Creativity and graduate education. *Molecular Biology of the Cell, 4,* 565–568.

Petrosko, J. M. (1978). Measuring creativity in elementary school: The current state of the art. *Journal of Creative Behavior, 12,* 109–119.

Piirto, J. (1999). A survey of psychological studies in creativity. In A. S. Fishkin, B. Cramond, & P. Olszewski-Kubilius (Eds.), *Investigating creativity in youth* (pp. 27–48). Creskill, NJ: Hampton Press.

Poincaré, H. (1995). *O valor da ciência* [The value of science]. Rio de Janeiro, Brazil: Contraponto. (Original work published 1911)

Poincaré, H. (1996). A invenção matemática [The invention of mathematics]. In P. Abrantes, L. C. Leal, & J. P. Ponte (Eds.), *Investigar para aprender matemática* [To investigate for learning mathematics] (pp. 7–14). Lisboa, Brazil: Projecto MPT & APM. (Original work published 1908)

Puccio, G. J. (1999). Creative problem solving preferences: Their identification and implications. *Creativity and Innovation Management, 8,* 171–178.

Puccio, G. J., Wheeler, R. A., & Cassander, V. J. (2004). Reactions to creative problem solving training: Does cognitive style make a difference? *Journal of Creative Behavior, 38,* 192–216.

Reigeluth, C. M., & Moore, J. (1999). Cognitive education and the cognitive domain. In C. H. Reigeluth (Ed.), *Instructional-design theories and models: A new paradigm of instructional theory* (Vol. II, pp. 51–68). London, England: LEA.

Renzulli, J. S. (1992). A general theory for the development of creative productivity through the pursuit of ideal acts of learning. *Gifted Child Quarterly, 36,* 170–182.

Renzulli, J. S., Smith, L. H., White, A. J., Callahan, C. M., Hartman, R. K., & Westberg, K. L. (2000). *Scales for rating the behavioral characteristics of superior students* [Revised ed.]. Waco, TX: Prufrock Press.

Ribeiro, R. A., & Fleith, D. S. (2007). O estímulo à criatividade em cursos de licenciatura [The incentive to creativity in training teachers' courses]. *Paidéia, Cadernos de Psicologia e Educação, 38,* 413–416.

Rickards, T., & Jones, L. (1991). Toward the identification of situational barriers to creative behaviors: The development of a self-report inventory. *Creativity Research Journal, 4,* 303–315.

Rimm, S., Davis, G. A., & Bien, Y. (1982). Identifying creativity: A characteristic approach. *Gifted Child Quarterly, 26,* 165–171.

Rogers, C. R. (1959). Toward a theory of creativity. In H. H. Anderson (Ed.), *Creativity and its cultivation* (pp. 69–82). New York, NY: Harper & Row.

Rosas, A. (1985). *Universidade e criatividade* [University and creativity]. Proceedings of the VII National Conference on Giftedness, 121–124.

Runco, M. A. (2004). Creativity. *Annual Review of Psychology, 55,* 657–687.

Runco, M. A. (2007). *Creativity: Theories and themes: Research, development, and practice.* Burlington, MA: Elsevier.

Rush, R. R., Denny, D. A., & Ives, S. (1967). Fostering creativity in the 6th grade and its effect on achievement. *Journal of Experimental Education, 36,* 80–86.

Sathler, T. C. (2007). *Desenvolvimento da criatividade na educação a distância segundo a percepção de universitários* [The development of creativity in online education according to university students] (Unpublished master's thesis). University of Brasilia, Brasilia, Brazil.

Schwartz, J. (1992). *O momento criativo. Mito e alienação na ciência moderna* [The creative moment. Myth and alienation in modern science]. São Paulo, Brazil: Best Seller.

Selby, E. C., Treffinger, D. J., Isaksen, S. G., & Lauer, K. J. (2004). Defining and assessing problem-solving style: Design and development of a new tool. *Journal of Creative Behavior, 38,* 221–243.

Shallcross, D. J. (1981). *Teaching creative behavior.* Englewood Cliffs, NJ: Prentice-Hall.

Sheffield, L. J. (2003). *Using creativity techniques to add depth and complexity to the mathematics curricula.* Retrieved from http://euler.math.ecnu.edu.cn/earcome3/sym1/EARCOME3_Sheffield_Linda_Sym1.doc

Siegel, S. M., & Kaemmerer, W. F. (1978). Measuring the perceived support for innovation in organizations. *Journal of Applied Psychology, 63,* 553–562.

Silva, J. S. (2003). A mudança de época e o contexto global cambiante: implicações para a mudança institucional em organizações de desenvolvimento [The change of epoch and the changing global context: Implications for institutional change in development organizations]. In S. M. V. Lima (Ed.), *Mudança organizacional: Teoria e gestão* [Organizational change: Theory and management] (pp. 65–110). Rio de Janeiro, Brazil: FGV.

Silva, P. A. (2000). *Criatividade do professor no ensino médio* [Teacher creativity in the secondary school] (Unpublished master's thesis). Catholic University of Campinas, Brazil.

Silver, E. A. (1985). *Teaching and learning mathematical problem solving: Multiple research perspectives.* Hillsdale, NJ: Erlbaum.

Silver, E. A. (1994). On mathematical problem posing. *For the Learning of Mathematics, 14,* 19–28.

Silver, E. A. (1997). Fostering creativity through instruction rich in mathematical problem solving and problem posing. *International Reviews on Mathematical Education, 29,* 75–80.

Silver, E. A., & Cai, J. (1996). An analysis of arithmetic problem posing by middle school students. *Journal for Research in Mathematics Education, 27,* 521–539.

Simonton, D. K. (2006). Creativity around the world in 80 ways . . . but with one destination. In J. C. Kaufman & R. J. Sternberg (Eds.), *The international handbook of creativity* (pp. 490–496). New York, NY: Cambridge University.

Singh, B. (1987). The development of tests to measure mathematical creativity. *International Journal of Mathematical Education in Science and Technology, 18,* 181–186.

Smith, G. T., & McCarthy, D. M. (1995). Methodological considerations in the refinement of clinical assessment instruments. *Psychological Assessment, 7,* 300–308.

Smith, L. R. (1990). Areas and perimeters of geoboard polygons. *Mathematics Teacher, 83,* 392–398.

Smith-Bingham, R. (2006). Public policy, innovation and the need for creativity. In N. Jackson, M. Oliver, M. Shaw, & J. Wisdom (Eds.), *Developing creativity in higher education* (pp. 10–18). London, England: Routledge.

Soh, K. C. (2000). Indexing creativity fostering teacher behavior: A preliminary validation study. *Journal of Creative Behavior, 34,* 118–132.

Sriraman, B. (2004). The characteristics of mathematical creativity. *The Mathematics Educator, 14,* 19–34.

Starko, A. J. (1995). *Creativity in the classroom.* White Plains, NY: Longman.

Sternberg, R. J. (1991, July). *A theory of creativity.* Paper presented at the XIV ISPA Colloquium, Braga, Portugal.

Sternberg, R. J. (2000). Identifying and developing creative giftedness. *Roeper Review, 23,* 60–64.

Sternberg, R. J. (2003). *Wisdom, intelligence, and creativity synthesized.* New York, NY: Cambridge University Press.

Sternberg, R. J., & Lubart, T. I. (1995). *Defying the crowd. Cultivating creativity in a culture of conformity.* New York, NY: The Free Press.

Sternberg, R. J., & Lubart, T. I. (1996). Investing in creativity. *American Psychologist, 51,* 677–688.

Strom, R. D., & Strom, P. S. (2002). Changing the rules: Education for creative thinking. *Journal of Creative Behavior, 36,* 183–200.

Tabachnick, B. G., & Fidell, S. (1996). *Using multivariate statistics* (3rd ed.). New York, NY: HarperCollins.

Tabachnick, B. G., & Fidell, L. S. (2001). *Using multivariate statistics.* Boston, MA: Allyn & Bacon.

Talbot, R. J. (1993). Creativity in the organizational context: Implications for training. In S. G. Isaksen, M. C. Murdock, R. L. Firestien, & D. J. Treffinger (Eds.), *Nurturing and developing creativity: The emergence of a discipline* (pp. 177–214). Norwood, NJ: Ablex.

Tan, A. G. (2001). Singaporean teachers' perceptions of activities useful for fostering creativity. *Journal of Creative Behavior, 35,* 131–148.

Tannenbaum, A. J. (1983). *Gifted children: Psychological and educational perspectives.* New York, NY: MacMillan.

Taylor, L. A. (1959). The nature of the creative process. In P. Smith (Ed.), *Creativity: An examination of the creative process.* New York, NY: Hartings House.

Tierney, P., & Farmer, S. M. (2004). Creative self-efficacy: Its potential antecedents and relationship to creative performance. *Academy of Management Journal, 45,* 1137–1148.

Tobias, S. (2004, May). *Fostering creativity in the science and mathematics classroom.* Paper presented at the National Science Foundation Conference, Malaysia. Retrieved from http://www.Wpi.edu/News/Events/SENM/tobias.ppt

Tolliver, J. M. (1985). Creativity at university. *Gifted Education International, 3,* 32–35.

Torrance, E. P. (1962). *Guiding creative talent.* Englewood Cliffs, NJ: Prentice-Hall.

Torrance, E. P. (1963). *Education and the creative potential.* Minneapolis: University of Minnesota Research Bureau.

Torrance, E. P. (1966). *Torrance Tests of Creative Thinking: Norms-technical manual.* Princeton, NJ: Personnel Press.

Torrance, E. P. (1970). *Encouraging creativity in the classroom.* Dubuque, IA: William C. Brown.

Torrance, E. P. (1974). *Torrance tests of creative thinking: Norms-technical manual.* Bensenville, IL: Scholastic Testing Service.

Torrance, E. P. (1987). Teaching for creativity. In S. G. Isaksen (Ed.), *Frontiers of creativity research: Beyond the basics* (pp. 189–215). Buffalo, NY: Bearly.

Torrance, E. P. (1988). The nature of creativity as manifest in its testing. In R. J. Sternberg (Ed.), *The nature of creativity: Contemporary psychological perspectives* (pp. 43–75). Cambridge, England: Cambridge University Press.

Torrance, E. P. (1990). *Torrance tests of creative thinking. Figural forms A and B.* Bensenville, IL: Scholastic Testing Service.

Torrance, E. P. (1995). *Why fly? A philosophy of creativity.* Norwood, NJ: Ablex.

Torrance, E. P., & Khatena, J. (1970). What kind of person are you? *Gifted Child Quarterly, 14,* 71–76.

Treffinger, D. J. (1987). Research on creativity assessment. In S. G. Isaksen (Ed.), *Frontiers of creativity research: Beyond the basics* (pp. 103–119). Buffalo, NY: Bearly.

Treffinger, D. J. (2003). Assessment and measurement in creativity and creative problem solving. In J. Houtz (Ed.), *The educational psychology of creativity* (pp. 59–93). Cresskill, NJ: Hampton Press.

Urban. K. K., & Jellen, H. G. (1996). *Tests for Creative Drawing Production (TCT-DP).* Lisse, Netherlands: Swets and Zeitlinger.

VanDemark, N. L. (1991). *Breaking the barriers in everyday creativity.* Buffalo, NY: The Creative Education Foundation.

Vasconcelos, M. C. (2002). *Um estudo sobre o incentivo e o desenvolvimento do raciocínio lógico dos alunos através da estratégia de resolução de problemas* [A study on the incentive and development of students' logical thinking through solving problems strategies] (Unpublished doctoral dissertation). Federal University of Santa Catarina, Florianópolis, Brazil.

Warr, P., & Allan, C. (1998). Learning strategies and occupational training. In C. L. Cooper & I. T. Robertson (Eds.), *International review of industrial and organizational psychology* (pp. 84–121). London, England: John Wiley & Sons.

Warr, P., & Downing, J. (2000). Learning strategies, learning anxiety and knowledge acquisition. *British Journal of Psychology, 91,* 331–333.

Wechsler, S. M. (2002). *Avaliação da criatividade por figuras e palavras. Testes de Torrance* [Creativity assessment by pictures and words. Torrance tests]. Campinas, Brazil: LAMP/PUC.

Wechsler, S. M. (2006a). *Estilos de pensar e criar* [Thinking and creativity styles]. Campinas, Brazil: LAMP/PUC.

Wechsler, S. M. (2006b). Validity of the Torrance Tests of Creative Thinking to the Brazilian culture. *Creativity Research Journal, 18,* 15–25.

Whitaker, D. C. A. (1995). Menino-menina: Sexo ou gênero? Alguns aspectos cruciais [Boy-girl: Sex or gender? Some important issues]. In R. V. Severino & M. A. R. L. Grande (Eds.), *A escola e seus alunos: Estudos sobre a diversidade cultural* [The school and its students: Studies on cultural diversity]. São Paulo, Brazil: EDUNESP.

Zerbini, T. (2003). *Estratégias de aprendizagem, reações aos procedimentos de um curso via Internet, reações ao tutor e impacto do treinamento no trabalho* [Learning strategies, reactions to internet training procedures, reactions to the tutor and impact of training on the job] (Unpublished master's thesis). University of Brasilia, Brazil.

Zhou, J., & Shalley, C. E. (2008). *Handbook of organizational creativity.* New York, NY: Lawrence Erlbaum.

Zimmerman, B. J. (2000). Self-efficacy: An essential motive to learn. *Contemporary Educational Psychology, 25,* 82–91.

Zwick, R., & Velicer, W. (1986). Comparison of five rules for determining the number of components to retain. *Psychological Bulletin, 99,* 432–442.

OBSTACLES TO PERSONAL CREATIVITY INVENTORY

I would be more creative if . . .

This questionnaire aims at the identification of factors that affect the expression of creativity. It includes a series of sentences that reflect these factors. Your task is to answer each item of the questionnaire, using the following scale:

1	2	3	4	5
Totally Disagree	Slightly Disagree	Unsure	Slightly Agree	Totally Agree

Mark one of the numbers next to each item with an "X" in accordance with the criteria defined above. Please, choose only one answer for each item and please respond to all items.

I would be more creative if . . .

1. I believed more in myself.	1	2	3	4	5
2. I were less shy to express my ideas.	1	2	3	4	5
3. I were more spontaneous.	1	2	3	4	5
4. I were not so critical of myself.	1	2	3	4	5
5. I were not so insecure.	1	2	3	4	5

6. I were not inclined to take risks.	1	2	3	4	5
7. I were not afraid of making mistakes.	1	2	3	4	5
8. I were more courageous.	1	2	3	4	5
9. I had more initiative.	1	2	3	4	5
10. I were not afraid of going against other people's ideas.	1	2	3	4	5
11. I were not so laid back.	1	2	3	4	5
12. I were less lazy.	1	2	3	4	5
13. I had more motivation to create.	1	2	3	4	5
14. I were more organized.	1	2	3	4	5
15. I had more time.	1	2	3	4	5
16. I were not afraid of facing the unknown.	1	2	3	4	5
17. I were a better observer.	1	2	3	4	5
18. there were more recognition of the creative work.	1	2	3	4	5
19. I exercised more the habit of searching for new ideas.	1	2	3	4	5
20. I were not afraid of facing criticism.	1	2	3	4	5
21. I were not afraid of expressing what I think.	1	2	3	4	5
22. I had been more motivated by my teachers.	1	2	3	4	5
23. I let loose my imagination.	1	2	3	4	5
24. I expressed my ideas better.	1	2	3	4	5
25. I were not afraid of carrying out my ideas.	1	2	3	4	5
26. I were more extroverted.	1	2	3	4	5
27. I were less perfectionistic.	1	2	3	4	5
28. I did not have feelings of inferiority in relation to others.	1	2	3	4	5
29. I took better advantage of the opportunities to exercise my creativity.	1	2	3	4	5
30. I were not afraid of being misunderstood.	1	2	3	4	5
31. I had more time to elaborate my ideas.	1	2	3	4	5
32. I had not been cut short by my family.	1	2	3	4	5
33. I were more intelligent.	1	2	3	4	5
34. I had more opportunities to put my ideas into practice.	1	2	3	4	5

	1	2	3	4	5
35. I had more incentive from my colleagues.	1	2	3	4	5
36. I were not afraid of what other people would think about me.	1	2	3	4	5
37. I had more opportunities to explore my potential.	1	2	3	4	5
38. I had not had a strict upbringing.	1	2	3	4	5
39. I had more opportunities to access information.	1	2	3	4	5
40. I had more freedom to express what I think.	1	2	3	4	5
41. I had more resources (equipments, books, money, etc.) to put my ideas into practice.	1	2	3	4	5
42. I had not been trimmed by my teachers.	1	2	3	4	5
43. I had had more opportunity to make mistakes without being labeled an idiot.	1	2	3	4	5
44. I were less criticized.	1	2	3	4	5
45. I were more persistent.	1	2	3	4	5
46. my ideas were more valued.	1	2	3	4	5
47. I ignored the criticism about my ideas.	1	2	3	4	5
48. there were more cooperation between people.	1	2	3	4	5
49. I valued my ideas more.	1	2	3	4	5
50. there were less competition among people.	1	2	3	4	5
51. I were more encouraged to speak my mind.	1	2	3	4	5
52. there were more acceptance of fantasy where I live.	1	2	3	4	5
53. people valued new ideas more.	1	2	3	4	5
54. there were more respect regarding the differences among people.	1	2	3	4	5
55. I were less bossy.	1	2	3	4	5
56. I were less fearful of ridicule.	1	2	3	4	5
57. I were not so critical in relation to other people's ideas.	1	2	3	4	5
58. I were more dedicated to what I do.	1	2	3	4	5
59. I had more energy.	1	2	3	4	5
60. I had more sense of humor.	1	2	3	4	5
61. I were less dependent on other people.	1	2	3	4	5
62. I had more ideas.	1	2	3	4	5
63. I concentrated more on the tasks I do.	1	2	3	4	5

64. I were more curious.	1	2	3	4	5
65. I were more enthusiastic.	1	2	3	4	5
66. I were more knowledgeable.	1	2	3	4	5

Gender: [ ] Male   [ ] Female   **Age:** _____ years

Level of education: _____

Profession: _____

THANK YOU VERY MUCH!

CLASSROOM CLIMATE FOR CREATIVITY SCALE

Mark an X next to the answer that applies to you:

I am a: ( ) boy ( ) girl   I am in the: ( ) third grade ( ) fourth grade

Age: _____ years

The name of my school is:_____

Date: _____/_____/_____

The sentences you will read in this questionnaire are related to what happens in your classroom. You should mark an X on the face that best shows what happens in your classroom. Choose only one face for each sentence and do not leave any questions unanswered.

See the example below:

	Never	Rarely	Sometimes	Often	Always
I play games.	☺	☺	☺	☺	☺

If you often play games in your classroom, you should mark an X on the face that says "often".

	Never	Rarely	Sometimes	Often	Always
I play games.	☺	☺	☺	✗	☺

Let's practice:

Read the sentences below and think: Which face best shows what happens in my classroom?

	Never	Rarely	Sometimes	Often	Always
I work in a group.	☺	☺	☺	☺	☺
I draw.	☺	☺	☺	☺	☺

In my classroom:	Never ☺	Rarely ☺	Sometimes ☺	Often ☺	Always ☺
1. The teacher pays attention to my ideas.					
2. I have a chance to participate in many activities.					
3. My ideas are welcome.					
4. I try to do things in different ways.					
5. The teacher asks me to show my work to other students.					
6. I think I'm creative.					
7. The teacher gives me enough time to think about a story I have to write.					
8. I use my imagination.					
9. Work is fun.					
10. I have many ideas.					
11. When I start a task, I like to finish it.					
12. The teacher cares about what I have to say.					
13. I like the content taught.					
14. The teacher asks me to think of new ideas.					
15. I learn about things I really like.					

In my classroom:	Never ☺	Rarely ☺	Sometimes ☺	Often ☺	Always ☺
16. I can make choices about what I want to do.					
17. I get so interested in my schoolwork that I do not know what is happening around me.					
18. I learn many things.					
19. The teacher asks me to try when I don't know the answer to a question.					
20. I am proud of myself.					
21. The teacher asks me to think of many ideas.					
22. I use books for research when I want to know more about a topic.					

TEACHING PRACTICES INVENTORY

QUESTIONNAIRE

Gender: ( ) Male   ( ) Female

Age:_____years _____months

Course: _____

University: _____

Number of course credits this semester: _____

Number of semesters:_____

Instructions

This questionnaire aims to identify university students' opinion regarding classroom practices typical of higher education professors.

With this purpose, we request your cooperation by responding with sincerity to all items, taking into account the practices of your professor in the _____ class.

You should express your opinion, based on a scale from 1 to 5.

If you strongly agree, considering, for example, that an item reflects a typical behavior or characteristic of your professor in the referred class, circle the number 5 on that particular item. If, however, you completely disagree with that behavior as typical of your professor, that is, that the item expressed a conduct which is rarely or never presented by your professor, you should circle the number 1.

The scale values are:

1	2	3	4	5
Strongly Disagree	Disagree	Unsure	Agree	Strongly Agree

Your responses will be treated confidentially and the results will be presented so as not to identify your responses.

Remarks:
- Please, give one answer only for each item.
- Answer all questions.
- For each question, give the first answer that occurs to you.

Thank you for your cooperation!

In general, the professor in my _____ class:

		Strongly Disagree	Disagree	Unsure	Agree	Strongly Agree
1	Cultivates in students interest concerning new discoveries and new knowledge.	1	2	3	4	5
2	Asks challenging questions that motivate students to think and to reason.	1	2	3	4	5
3	Encourages students to examine different aspects of a problem.	1	2	3	4	5
4	Encourages students' initiative.	1	2	3	4	5
5	Encourages students to think of new ideas regarding the content of the discipline.	1	2	3	4	5
6	Promotes students' self-confidence.	1	2	3	4	5
7	Stimulates students' curiosity through the proposed tasks.	1	2	3	4	5

		Strongly Disagree	Disagree	Unsure	Agree	Strongly Agree
8	Encourages students' independence.	1	2	3	4	5
9	Develops students' critical analysis skills.	1	2	3	4	5
10	Guides students to know and understand differing points of view on the same issue or topic of study.	1	2	3	4	5
11	Values students' original ideas.	1	2	3	4	5
12	Encourages students to ask questions concerning the topics studied.	1	2	3	4	5
13	Is solely concerned with the information content.	1	2	3	4	5
14	Creates an environment of respect and acceptance of students' ideas.	1	2	3	4	5
15	Provides students a chance to disagree with the teacher's points of view.	1	2	3	4	5
16	Uses evaluation strategies that require only the reproduction of content given in class or in the adopted books.	1	2	3	4	5
17	Presents various aspects of an issue that is being studied.	1	2	3	4	5
18	Always uses the same teaching method.	1	2	3	4	5
19	Promotes debate to encourage the participation of all students.	1	2	3	4	5
20	Asks questions, seeking connections to the topics studied.	1	2	3	4	5
21	Uses examples to illustrate the content taught in class.	1	2	3	4	5
22	Is ready to clear students' doubts.	1	2	3	4	5
23	Provides extensive bibliography on the topics covered.	1	2	3	4	5
24	Arouses the students' interest through the content being taught.	1	2	3	4	5
25	Is available to meet students outside the classroom.	1	2	3	4	5
26	Makes use of diversified strategies of evaluation.	1	2	3	4	5
27	Presents problem situations to be resolved by students.	1	2	3	4	5
28	Exposes the contents in a didactic manner.	1	2	3	4	5
29	Provides students little choice about the assignments to be developed.	1	2	3	4	5
30	Gives constructive feedback to students.	1	2	3	4	5
31	Offers important and interesting information regarding the academic discipline content.	1	2	3	4	5
32	Has enthusiasm toward the content taught.	1	2	3	4	5
33	Listens carefully to students' interventions.	1	2	3	4	5

		Strongly Disagree	Disagree	Unsure	Agree	Strongly Agree
34	Is not attentive to the students' interests.	1	2	3	4	5
35	Has positive expectations regarding students' performance.	1	2	3	4	5
36	Has a sense of humor in the classroom.	1	2	3	4	5
37	Presents updated content.	1	2	3	4	5

INDICATORS OF THE CLIMATE FOR CREATIVITY IN THE WORKPLACE

Factors and Respective Items Making Up the Indicators of Climate for Creativity

Factors Related to Stimuli to Creativity

Factor 1—Appropriate Physical Environment

29. I have the furniture I need in my workplace.
47. I have sufficient physical space to keep my working materials.
4. Lighting in my workplace is appropriate.
9. I have the material resources I need to do my work.
40. I have the necessary technological resources for my job, such as a personal computer.
87. Noise in the workplace affects the performance of my tasks.
51. The physical space in the workplace is insufficient for the number of staff.
8. The ambient temperature at my workplace is inadequate.
83. Necessary equipment is lacking in my workplace for the activities I perform.
15. Getting the materials I need to carry out my tasks is a slow process.

Factor 2—Positive Social Environment Among Work Colleagues

58. The climate among colleagues is one of confidence and mutual respect.

28. In my working group, people are willing to help one another.
55. The relaxed atmosphere in my working group facilitates a positive relationship between staff.
68. People in my working group take responsibility for the tasks they carry out.
57. There is excessive competition among the members of my working group.
85. My colleagues get jealous when I am more requested to do things by my superiors then they are.
10. There's a lot of rivalry between different groups in my organization.
66. Coming up with a new idea in my working group is seen as a show-offish attitude of the person suggesting it.
60. When I propose a new idea, there's always someone who presents it as his or her own later.

Factor 3—Incentives to New Ideas
82. My colleagues at work encourage me to come up with new ideas.
80. My working group encourages each of its members to speak his or her mind.
52. I am encouraged to face challenges in search of new solutions for problems.
77. My boss or bosses congratulate me when I do a good job.
5. My boss or bosses encourage their subordinates to look for new ideas and solutions for problems faced by the organization.
70. Meetings to evaluate actions are held.
35. I am requested to suggest improvements to the services provided to clients.
19. People are encouraged to experiment with new ways of doing their job.
14. My immediate boss doesn't hold meetings with his or her staff to discuss problems in the department.

Factor 4—Freedom of Action
38. I feel comfortable acting in different ways than my colleagues.
34. I feel comfortable acting in different ways than my boss or bosses.
25. I am free to decide how to carry out the tasks assigned to me.
16. In my working group, I am free to express my ideas.
18. I feel comfortable expressing my ideas to my colleagues at work, regardless of how ridiculous they might seem.
90. I am free to question orders.

1. My superiors have confidence in my work.
44. My boss or bosses accept ideas that are different from theirs.
49. People who make mistakes are humiliated by their bosses.
89. I feel like I'm being watched while going about my work.

Factor 5—Challenging Activities

24. The tasks I carry out in my workplace require the best of me.
96. I feel the need to look for new knowledge to fulfill the tasks assigned to me.
12. I feel that I do important work for the organization.
88. Some tasks require that I create new ways of carrying them out.
72. The tasks assigned to me require a lot of effort.
93. I have the habit of discussing ideas with my colleagues to find solutions to daily problems.

Factor 6—Adequate Salaries and Benefits

81. My wages are consistent with my job.
62. My organization offers staff development programs.
17. My salary motivates me to work.
86. Staff development programs meet the needs of the employees.
42. The organization rewards high-performing staff.
45. In my organization, innovative ideas are rewarded.
13. The organization where I work provides training courses designed to develop the creative potential of its staff.
32. I am pleased with the promotion policy of this organization.

Factor 7—Actions by Managers and the Organization in Support of New Ideas

5. My boss or bosses encourage staff to look for new ideas and solutions for problems faced by the organization.
63. In my organization, work targets are clear and well-defined.
41. My boss or bosses appreciate individual contributions from staff.
30. My boss or bosses state very clearly what they expect from me.
3. My initiatives are appreciated in my workplace.
6. I get appropriate guidance for carrying out tasks under my responsibility.
27. People in senior levels in my organization believe in the creative capacity of its staff.
2. One of the targets of the organization is seeking innovation.
50. My boss or bosses criticize staff constructively.

84. Meetings are held to seek joint solutions for problems.
77. My boss or bosses congratulate me when I do a good job.
70. Meetings to evaluate actions are held.
44. My boss or bosses accept ideas that are different from theirs.

Factor 8—Availability of Material Resources
9. I have the material resources I need to do my work.
40. I have the necessary technological resources for my job, such as a phone and a fax machine.
74. In my workplace, I have the information I need to carry out my tasks.
83. Necessary equipment is lacking in my workplace for the activities I perform.

Factors Related to Barriers to Creativity

Factors 1—Blocking of New Ideas
76. My immediate boss blocks my initiatives in the workplace.
67. Bosses see their solutions to problems as more appropriate.
60. When I propose a new idea, there's always someone who presents it as his or her own later.
53. My immediate boss fears that I might have a better performance than his or hers in the workplace.
66. Coming up with a new idea in my working group is seen as a show-offish attitude of the person suggesting it.
64. I am not free to decide how I should carry out my tasks.
61. Where I work, people get so attached to their jobs that they forget what the goals of the organization are all about.

Factor 2—Excessive Number of Tasks and Scarcity of Time
79. Excessive tasks prevent me from having the time to reflect on the best way to carry them out.
73. The activities under my responsibility require more time than I have.
21. The deadlines for performing tasks are very short.
97. Short deadlines for carrying out tasks jeopardize their quality.
36. Excessive work prevents me from attending training courses held in this organization.
11. I don't have time to experiment with new ways of working.
65. To complete my tasks within schedule, I have to work overtime at home.
72. The tasks assigned to me require a lot of effort.

95. The rules applied to my work routine make it difficult for me to do my job.
48. My organization gives me the time I need to develop new ideas.
31. Staff is lacking to implement projects.

Factor 3—Resistance to New Ideas

22. Bosses don't take the risk of trying out new working alternatives.
20. Older staff members in the organization resist accepting suggestions from newer employees.
33. Staff members who disagree with their bosses are not seen favorably.
23. People with different opinions inside the group are not well accepted.
26. Training programs are only available to senior staff.
 7. To be successful in the organization, employees must be friends with or related to the boss.
39. My colleagues think I'm taking a risk when I try and come up with a new idea in the working group.
37. Staff are accustomed to receiving orders and not to coming up with new ideas.

Factor 4—Organizational Problems

92. To implement a new idea, approval at various levels is required.
75. There are too many instructions and rules to be followed.
91. Political problems affect efficiency in my organization.
43. There's too much red tape in the organization where I work.
56. There are communication problems between the units that create the rules and those that apply them.
46. People in my organization are concerned with protecting their "turfs."
94. People worry too much about negative criticism of their work.
54. Traditions and rules make it difficult to introduce innovations.
59. In their tasks, people repeat models that have been in use for a long time.
78. All change efforts are met with resistance.
71. For political reasons, projects are rejected.
69. It is considered risky to take chances.

STRATEGIES FOR CREATING AT WORK

This research concerns what you do to have new ideas in order to solve daily problems in your work. Read attentively the following items and indicate the score that best represents your opinion on the strategies you use in your work. The scale varies from 1 (never) to 10 (always). Please do not leave questions without an answer.

ITEMS	Never									Always
1. To express my opinion on a work issue I gather varied information about it.	1	2	3	4	5	6	7	8	9	10
2. I make a mental list of possible solutions to a problem at work.	1	2	3	4	5	6	7	8	9	10
3. When I reflect on solutions to a problem, I think how they would affect other areas of my work.	1	2	3	4	5	6	7	8	9	10
4. When analyzing a problem at work, I think about how I might redefine it.	1	2	3	4	5	6	7	8	9	10
5. When I am pressed for ideas at work, I seek ways to reduce the pressure.	1	2	3	4	5	6	7	8	9	10
6. I reflect on how to best implement an idea about work.	1	2	3	4	5	6	7	8	9	10
7. Even after I have mastered a work subject, I strive to see it in new ways.	1	2	3	4	5	6	7	8	9	10

ITEMS	Never									Always
8. When I have an idea at work, I often wonder what would be its consequences on other activities in my sector.	1	2	3	4	5	6	7	8	9	10
9. I read up on several topics to inspire me to have new ideas about work.	1	2	3	4	5	6	7	8	9	10
10. When anxiety stops me from having ideas at work, I try to relax and think about good things.	1	2	3	4	5	6	7	8	9	10
11. To better understand a work problem, I try to collect information from various sources.	1	2	3	4	5	6	7	8	9	10
12. At work, I intercalate moments of intense activity in problem solving with moments of fun and relaxation.	1	2	3	4	5	6	7	8	9	10
13. To have ideas at work, I keep myself updated by reading articles and texts about my area of expertise.	1	2	3	4	5	6	7	8	9	10
14. For work, I consider the most diverse ideas that come to mind, even if they may seem inappropriate at first.	1	2	3	4	5	6	7	8	9	10
15. When I cannot find a solution to a problem at work, I "give it a rest."	1	2	3	4	5	6	7	8	9	10
16. To have different ideas at work, I pretend to know nothing about a subject.	1	2	3	4	5	6	7	8	9	10
17. I imagine the perfect solution to a problem at work, even if it is fantastical.	1	2	3	4	5	6	7	8	9	10
18. I select the best sources of information about my activities, so I can access them when I have problems at work.	1	2	3	4	5	6	7	8	9	10
19. I refine the ideas I have at work, improving proposed solutions.	1	2	3	4	5	6	7	8	9	10
20. To solve a problem at work I try to combine different ideas.	1	2	3	4	5	6	7	8	9	10
21. When I cannot solve a work problem, I temporarily distract myself with other matters.	1	2	3	4	5	6	7	8	9	10

ITEMS	Never									Always
22. I seek to understand a work problem from different angles.	1	2	3	4	5	6	7	8	9	10
23. I play in my head with bizarre and unusual ideas about my work.	1	2	3	4	5	6	7	8	9	10
24. I evaluate the usefulness of the solutions that I find for a work problem.	1	2	3	4	5	6	7	8	9	10
25. To break the routine, I do my work in ways I am not accustomed to.	1	2	3	4	5	6	7	8	9	10
26. I use many approaches to reflect about a work topic.	1	2	3	4	5	6	7	8	9	10
27. I seek reading material on the work problem that I have to solve.	1	2	3	4	5	6	7	8	9	10
28. I combine different perspectives in generating ideas about my work.	1	2	3	4	5	6	7	8	9	10
29. When I try to resolve an issue at work I contemplate it for extended periods of time	1	2	3	4	5	6	7	8	9	10
30. I think about many different ways to accomplish a task at work.	1	2	3	4	5	6	7	8	9	10
31. I talk about work problems with people with interests similar to mine.	1	2	3	4	5	6	7	8	9	10
32. I check whether the methods that I know apply to solving new problems at work.	1	2	3	4	5	6	7	8	9	10
33. I try to reformulate a work problem to better understand it.	1	2	3	4	5	6	7	8	9	10
34. I put together different ideas to solve work problems.	1	2	3	4	5	6	7	8	9	10
35. When analyzing a work problem, if necessary, I will change my initial opinion.	1	2	3	4	5	6	7	8	9	10
36. When I have a work problem to solve, I seek help from more experienced colleagues.	1	2	3	4	5	6	7	8	9	10
37. To better understand new situations at work, I look for things that are familiar to me.	1	2	3	4	5	6	7	8	9	10

ITEMS	Never									Always
38. When reflecting on possible solutions to a problem at work, I leave my criticism for later.	1	2	3	4	5	6	7	8	9	10
39. To better understand my tasks, I compare them with previous work experiences.	1	2	3	4	5	6	7	8	9	10
40. I recognize the limitations of my own ideas about my work.	1	2	3	4	5	6	7	8	9	10
41. I seek an isolated environment in order to focus only on the work problem I am analyzing.	1	2	3	4	5	6	7	8	9	10
42. I discuss the problem I'm solving with my coworkers.	1	2	3	4	5	6	7	8	9	10
43. I talk to myself mentally, encouraging myself to be creative at work.	1	2	3	4	5	6	7	8	9	10
44. I seek to create many alternative solutions to a problem.	1	2	3	4	5	6	7	8	9	10

ABOUT THE EDITORS

Eunice Soriano de Alencar, Ph.D., is professor emerita of psychology at the University of Brasília, Brazil and researcher for the National Council for Scientific and Technical Development. She has served as president of the Brazilian Association for the Gifted at the Federal District, and vice president of the Ibero-American Federation of the World Council for Gifted and Talented Children. For more than 40 years, she has carried out research projects and published several books and numerous book chapters and articles in professional journals, especially on giftedness and creativity. Among her books are *Psychology and Education of the Gifted, Psychology of Creativity, How to Develop the Creative Potential, Managing Creativity, The Child in the Family and in Society,* and *Creativity and the Education of the Gifted.* She is on the editorial board of several journals in Brazil and abroad and is a honorary member of the Brazilian Council for Giftedness.

Maria de Fátima Bruno-Faria, Ph.D., is a psychologist and an associate professor in the department of administration at the Federal University of Brasília, Brazil. She received her doctoral degree from the University of Rio de Janeiro in the area of creativity process in organizations. She is the author of numerous articles and book chapters on creativity in the workplace. Her research interests include creativity in organizations, organizational innovation, culture of innovation, and management of human resources. She is leader of the research group on creativity and innovation in organizations from the National Council for Scientific and Technical Development.

Denise de Souza Fleith, Ph.D., is a psychologist and an associate professor at the Institute of Psychology at University of Brasília, Brazil. She received her doctoral degree from the University of Connecticut in gifted and talented education. She is the author of books and articles on giftedness and creativity. Her research interests include gifted education, creativity, instrument development, and teacher training. She is a member of the Executive Committee of the World Council for Gifted and Talented Children and associate editor of the Brazilian journal *Psicologia: Teoria e Pesquisa* [Psychology: Theory and Research]. Denise has also served as tutor in the Tutorial Education Program, a Brazilian Honors' Program. In 1998, she received the NAGC Graduate Student Research Award from the Research and Evaluation Division.

ABOUT THE AUTHORS

Cleyton Hércules Gontijo, Ph.D., is an assistant professor at the University of Brasilia, Brazil. He currently serves as leader of the research group on Mathematics Education from the National Council for the Scientific and Technological Development.

Melissa Machado de Moraes, Ph.D., is a student at ESSEC Business School in France.

Suzana Maria Valle Lima, Ph.D., is a professor of the graduate program in Social Psychology, Organizational and Work at the Institute of Psychology, University of Brasilia. She is also a researcher at the Brazilian Agricultural Research Corporation and an international consultant on innovation management, organizational change, and strategy.